YOUR
PLASTIC
FOOTPRINT

YOUR PLASTIC FOOTPRINT

The Facts About Plastic Pollution and What You Can Do to Reduce Your Footprint

Rachel Salt

FIREFLY BOOKS

A FIREFLY BOOK

Published by Firefly Books Ltd. 2020
Copyright © 2020 Firefly Books Ltd.
Text copyright © 2020 Rachel Salt
Photographs © as listed on pages 154–155

First printing

Library of Congress Control Number: 2020939722

Library and Archives Canada Cataloguing in Publication
Title: Your plastic footprint : the facts about plastic and what you can do to reduce your footprint / Rachel Salt.
Names: Salt, Rachel, 1988- author.
Description: Includes bibliographical references and index.
Identifiers: Canadiana 20200262300 | ISBN 9780228102489 (hardcover) | ISBN 9780228103103 (softcover)
Subjects: LCSH: Plastic scrap—Environmental aspects. | LCSH: Plastics—Environmental aspects. | LCSH: Plastics industry and trade—Environmental aspects. | LCSH: Waste minimization. | LCSH: Nature—Effect of human beings on.
Classification: LCC TD798 .S26 2020 | DDC 363.72/88—dc23

Published in the United States by
Firefly Books (U.S.) Inc.
P.O. Box 1338, Ellicott Station
Buffalo, New York 14205

Published in Canada by
Firefly Books Ltd.
50 Staples Avenue, Unit 1
Richmond Hill, Ontario L4B 0A7

Cover and interior design: Hartley Millson
Cover image: smartboy10 / iStock
Charts and illustrations on pages 13, 20, 21, 23, 27, 30, 31, 34, 37, 38, 50, 63, 107: George A. Walker

Printed in Korea

 Canada We acknowledge the financial support of the Government of Canada.

(page 2) A rubber boot is washed up on the beach of Sand Island, Midway Atoll.

For Cameron

Contents

Introduction

Do you know how many pieces of plastic you dispose of in a day? Not sure? How about a year? Or even a lifetime? Probably not. Well, don't feel bad. Though plastic is an incredible material that is strong, flexible and inexpensive, we more often than not put it in the garbage without paying it much thought.

But those pieces — a candy wrapper, a water bottle, a polyester T-shirt (yes, over 60 percent of clothing is made from plastic) — really add up over time. The average American creates 2.58 kilograms (5.69 pounds) of waste a day, and 13 percent of that is plastic. That adds up to 37,729,383 kilograms (83,179,051 pounds) of plastic waste across America in a single day.

The impact from plastic waste is immense as it clogs our waterways and chokes marine life. Every year 8 million tons (over 17 billion pounds) of plastic enters the ocean. That would be equivalent to lining every foot of coastline with five grocery bags filled with plastic. However, the issue with plastic isn't just the trash it creates. Its production also takes a toll on our environment. This book examines not only the impact of plastic pollution as waste but also how its production generates carbon emissions and affects human health.

You will encounter some jarring numbers and images in the following pages, but this book isn't a story of dismay. It's a call to action, with guidance on how to analyze and reduce your plastic usage. If you can investigate how your plastic waste piles up — from items that can stay with you over a lifetime, such as a car or a beloved toy, to single-use items you throw away in a heartbeat, like a straw or a coffee cup — you can take conscious steps to reduce your reliance on plastic.

This book also aims to give you the ideas and resources you need to take action on a broader scale. We dissect the systems currently in place and give you a better understanding of the advantages and shortcomings of proposed solutions to the plastic problem.

What Is a Plastic Footprint?

A plastic footprint is a metric used to measure how much plastic your lifestyle contributes to the global trash pile. Think of a carbon footprint, but with all the plastic items you've interacted with over your lifetime.

We get into more specifics at the end of Chapters 4 and 5, but generally speaking a plastic footprint is measured by conducting a "plastic waste audit." This is a recorded list of how much plastic you throw away in a given period of time. This includes items you use over the long term, such as a laptop, to single-use items you use for a matter of minutes. From this, you can figure out how much plastic waste you throw away in a year and in your lifetime.

Your plastic footprint isn't a simple thing to measure, and a lot of your numbers will be generated from estimates based on how you currently use plastic items. The result might not consider times in your life when you were perhaps using less or more plastic, but the point of the exercise is to create a general picture of your plastic use.

Why Measure Your Footprint?

Because you can't manage what you don't measure. This book gives you the opportunity to assess where your plastic-use baseline is at and set you on a path to change it for the better. By examining our waste, we are forced to be mindful about the choices we make and what we throw away.

CHAPTER 1

Plastic 101

Plastic is so ubiquitous in our everyday lives that it's difficult imagining a world without it. But relatively speaking plastic has only been on the scene for a short while. When exactly was it invented? And also, what exactly is it? This chapter is your crash course on the origins of this unique invention.

The History of Plastic

Within the past 60 years, mass production of plastic has seen a meteoric rise, but its origins began over 150 years ago.

Billiard Balls

The surprising beginning of plastic production is linked to billiard (or pool) balls. In fact, without billiards we may never have had modern-day plastic. Pool was once a wildly popular activity. During the mid-19th century there were 830 pool halls in Chicago alone (today there are estimated to be fewer than

(left) A view over the Kern River Oil Field in Bakersfield, California. The vast majority of plastics are made from fossil fuels, such as oil.

1,400 in all of the United States). In those days pool balls were made from ivory, which came from the tusks of elephants. On average a tusk could only make three balls and consequently led to the death of an elephant. As demand for ivory grew, there was greater concern that elephants would soon become extinct, and billiard businesses worried there would be no ivory left to stock their pool tables. With this in mind, in 1863 Michael Phelan, considered the father of American billiards, put an ad in the paper offering $10,000 (equivalent to $3 million today) to whomever could find a suitable alternative to ivory.

Amateur inventor John Wesley Hyatt took up the challenge and created a completely new material dubbed celluloid. Synthesized from the cellulose in cotton, it is considered one of the first plastics. Unfortunately for Hyatt he didn't win the contest. Celluloid didn't make for very effective billiard balls as it lacked the bounce of ivory. Yet this material was versatile and found several other uses, including for combs and film.

Celluloid would inspire other plastic inventions. Bakelite (invented by Leo Baekeland in 1907) was the first fully synthetic plastic generated from fossil fuels.

World War II

During World War II, conserving resources was essential, and items such as natural rubber and silk were rationed. This ushered in an opportunity for synthetic materials.

Plastic production grew by 300 percent during the war. The military used plastic for parachutes, helmet liners, bazooka barrels and many other purposes. Even the atomic bomb contained plastic.

"Better Living . . . through Chemistry"

War facilitated the production and invention of several industrial plastic products, and in the decades that followed there was an era of mass consumption. The chemical company giant DuPont had the advertising slogan "Better Things for Better Living . . . through Chemistry," but it is also a phrase that helped define this time in history. Plastic allowed for the invention of endless products designed to make life easier for the modern person. It was cheap, sanitary, lightweight and considered safe. And above all it was capable of being molded into whatever we desired.

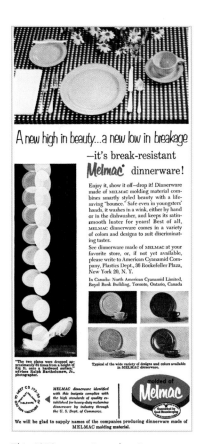

This 1950s magazine advertisement touts the durability and versatility of Melmac, a brand of dinnerware made from melamine resin.

Global Plastics Production 1950-2015

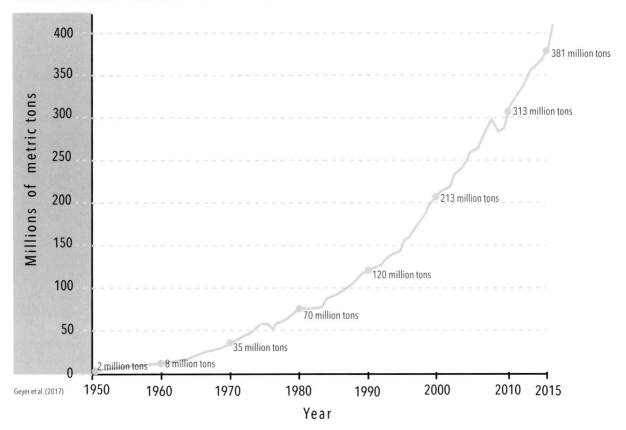

Geyer et al. (2017)

Since 1950, production of this "dream material" has grown 190 times globally. In 2017 the U.S. alone produced over 32 million metric tons (35.4 million U.S. tons) of plastic. But what exactly is modern plastic made of? The next section explores how plastic is created.

U.S. Tons vs. Metric Tons (Tonnes)

Different countries use different units of measurement. The United States uses the ton, or short ton, as a measure of mass while most of the world uses the metric ton (also known as a tonne). These measurements sound similar but have different values:

- **1 U.S. ton = 2,000 pounds (907.18 kilograms)**
- **1 metric ton = 2,204 pounds (1,000 kilograms)**
- **1 metric ton = 1.10231 U.S. tons**

The international system of units recognizes the metric ton, and these are the units most scientists use. For that reason, only metric tons will be used for the remainder of this book.

Fossil Fuels: The Origins of Plastic

Fossil fuels don't really come from fossils, but rather decomposed plants and animals that were buried under sand and rock. Over millions of years, the surrounding sand and rock create pressure and heat around the decaying plants and animals, which turn them into what we use as fuel.

Did you know that 99 percent of all plastic comes from fossil fuels? Though there is growing interest in bioplastics (plastic material produced from plants), the bulk of our plastic is still derived from oil and gas (and sometimes coal). The fossil fuel industry and the plastic industry are inextricably linked, so to understand plastic and its impact on our planet, it's important to learn about fossil fuels — how they're extracted, processed and transported across the globe.

Extracting

Extracting fossil fuel resources from the ground requires drilling. Drilling is the act of boring a hole into the ground to create a well for oil and gas. Companies don't simply drill a hole anywhere and expect to hit oil, rather the location of oil and gas is assessed by geologists via exploratory wells. Exploration can happen through seismic surveying (sound waves are bounced off underground rock formations that provide information about the rock types and possible gases and fluid below), core sampling (soil and rock samples can help give clues about possible reserves) and other technologies. Wells can be drilled on land and even in the middle of the ocean, through the seafloor.

Once a reserve is established a drill bit and pipe create a vertical hole in the ground. Sometimes, when a reserve is below a residential area, for example, drillers bore the hole at an angle. Next, a substance called "drilling mud" is circulated into the hole, which helps remove rock. Once the hole is the desired size and depth it is cased with cement to prevent collapsing. Small holes called perforations are then punched into portions of the casing to allow the crude oil or gas to flow into the well.

Can You Make Plastic from Coal?

The short answer is yes. It is possible to convert coal into the chemicals required to make plastic, but the process is extremely energy, water and emissions intensive. It is also quite costly. That is why this process is done almost exclusively in China, where there is an abundance of coal.

Shale gas, a type of natural gas, is removed through a process known as fracking. Fracking is a method of extracting natural gas from shale rock by injecting water and other chemicals at high pressures until it fractures the rock, releasing the gas.

Oil

In 2019 world oil production averaged over 80 million barrels per day. According to the World Economic Forum, plastic production accounts for roughly 4 to 8 percent of oil consumption. Of this percentage, half is used for the actual plastic products while the other half is used as energy to make the plastic. Even using the more conservative estimate of 4 percent, this means that over 3 million barrels of oil minimum are used each day worldwide to make plastic.

A barrel, often shortened to bbl, is a unit of volume for crude oil and other petroleum products. One barrel is equivalent to 42 U.S. gallons, or roughly 159 liters.

What Can You Get from One Barrel of Oil?

72 liters (19 gallons) of gasoline

SF   LA

519 kilometers

With this you could drive a midsized car 519 kilometers (323 miles), which is about the distance from San Francisco to Los Angeles.

15 liters (4 gallons) of jet fuel

4 seconds

This would provide approximately 4 seconds of flight (a Boeing 747 plane uses approximately a gallon every second).

8,500 plastic bags

× 8,500

1,700 kWh (kilowatt-hours)

This amount of energy is enough to charge your phone overnight for 242 years.

242 years

Natural Gas

Unlike crude oil, which is a liquid, natural gas is . . . a gas! So instead of barrels it is measured in cubic meters or feet. An estimated 3.9 trillion cubic meters (136.6 trillion cubic feet) was produced in 2018. Experts estimate that of this volume 1.8 percent is used to develop plastic, which means that each day 69.6 billion cubic meters (2.5 trillion cubic feet) of natural gas are used to make plastic. That is equivalent to over 28 million hot air balloons.

What exactly is natural gas made of? Natural gas is primarily methane but is also made of several other compounds. Below is the typical composition of natural gas.

When it comes to plastic, ethane is the most important raw material of natural gas. This gas is converted into ethylene through a process called "steam cracking." (More about this later.) Polymer chains of ethylene form polyethylene, the most common type of plastic used for packaging.

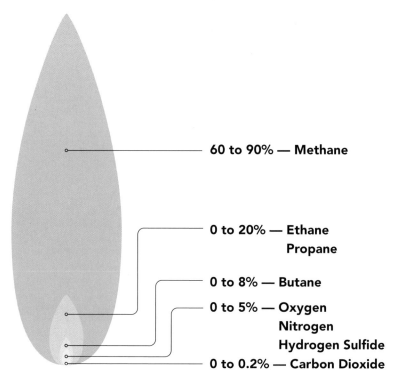

60 to 90% — Methane

**0 to 20% — Ethane
Propane**

0 to 8% — Butane

**0 to 5% — Oxygen
Nitrogen
Hydrogen Sulfide**

0 to 0.2% — Carbon Dioxide

Methane and Climate Change

Methane (CH_4) is a simple molecule composed of one carbon atom and four hydrogen atoms. It is also a powerful greenhouse gas with significant consequences for climate change. This gas has a greater impact on atmospheric warming than carbon dioxide (CO_2). In fact, within the first two decades of being released into the atmosphere, methane has shown to trap 84 times as much heat as CO_2. Scientists once believed that the bulk of methane emissions came from livestock, predominantly cattle farts and burps (seriously). Though the impacts from farming remain significant, recent research has concluded that fracking has played a major role in methane emissions and the subsequent climate emergency.

Transportation

Oil and natural gas reserves are extracted only in certain parts of the world but are consumed across the globe as fuel and to make products. How are the raw materials of plastic transported? Essentially, companies transport oil and gas four different ways: pipelines, ships, trains and trucks.

- **Pipelines.** The United States has the largest network of pipelines in the world. Here, 70 percent of crude oil and petroleum products are shipped by pipeline. If you lined up all of America's natural gas and oil pipelines, they would stretch for 3.9 million kilometers (2.4 million miles). Consider this: the distance to the moon is 384,472 kilometers (238,900 miles), meaning if you traveled the distance of the pipelines it would be equivalent to five trips to the moon and back.
- **Ships.** Internationally, 61 percent of fossil fuel (approximately 58 million barrels a day) travels by sea. By weight, oil tankers account for 28 percent of all the world's shipping. Long Range class ships are the most common type of oil tanker. A single Long Range tanker can handle between 310,000 and 550,000 barrels of crude oil.
- **Trains.** In 2018 over 200 million barrels of crude oil were transported by train, making up just 3 percent of shipments in the U.S.
- **Trucks.** Trucks transport oil and gas over short distances and account for 4 percent of oil and gas transport.

The Trans Alaska Pipeline runs 1,287.5 kilometers (800 miles) from Prudhoe Bay to Valdez, Alaska, and crosses three mountain ranges.

The carbon emissions created as a result of transporting oil and gas further contribute to plastic's impact on the environment. If disaster strikes during extraction or transportation, fossil fuels can have even more immediate and dire effects.

Drills and Spills

The building blocks of plastic can be messy to extract and transport and have resulted in spills with significant environmental consequences. Sadly, these events are fairly common and can originate at drilling sites and refineries, across pipelines and on ships. The extent of damage spills create depends on where the spill occurs and its chemical composition.

Contamination is usually much worse in water than on land because it is able to spread over a greater area with less effective containment, which impacts more species. Spills have a direct negative impact on animals and wildlife, particularly marine mammals and seabird species, which must continually pass through surface water to breathe. Spills can lead to ingestion of oil, oil accumulation in body tissues, DNA changes and damage, heart failure and the death of eggs and larvae.

Spills also impact wildlife indirectly. Marine ecosystems have complex structures, with species that interact and depend on one another. An increased mortality rate for one species as a result of a spill can create a cascading effect that can alter community structures of organisms, including predation, grazing patterns and competition dynamics.

When an oil spill happens, large crews assemble on shorelines to clean and scrub seabirds. Oil companies deploy booms to contain the spill, fire to burn the fuel, chemical dispersants to break down the oil into smaller pieces and skimmers to remove

A bird, covered in oil from the Gulf Oil Spill, struggles to climb over a boom in Barataria Bay, Louisiana.

Lac-Mégantic Rail Disaster

In July 2013, a train carrying approximately 8 million liters (over 2 million gallons) of crude oil derailed in the downtown area of Lac-Mégantic, Quebec. Nearly 6 million liters (1.6 million gallons) of oil leaked from the tankers, which resulted in an explosion that killed 47 people and destroyed a large part of the town. Roughly 100,000 liters (26,400 gallons) of oil leaked into the neighboring Chaudière River as well, creating concerns over the long-term impact on wildlife and communities downstream.

Deepwater Horizon and the Gulf Oil Spill

In April 2010 there was an explosion and fire on a BP oil rig in the Gulf of Mexico. The accident killed 11 workers and caused an estimated 4.9 million barrels of oil to flow into the ocean. Though the incident occurred on April 20, the company was unable cap the well until July 15 and permanently seal it until September 19.

The size and area of the spill is debated among scientists. Some argued that the bulk of the oil remained floating on the surface with just 10 percent making it to the shore. Still, this impacted over 1,600 kilometers (1,000 miles) of shoreline. Other scientists reported discovering a thick coating of oil at the bottom of the ocean across an area of 4,660 square kilometers (2,900 square miles) containing dead starfish and other organisms. One year after the spill the U.S. Fish and Wildlife Service recorded more than 6,100 dead seabirds, 600 dead sea turtles and 153 dead dolphins.

Boats try to battle the fire following the explosion of Deepwater Horizon.

the oil. But is any of this really effective? These containment methods can be somewhat helpful during small spills in calm sheltered waters but are entirely ineffective for large spills. For example, a study released by the City of Vancouver in 2015 concluded that if a large ship or pipeline spill occurred on the southern coast of British Columbia, collecting and removing the oil from the sea surface would be a challenging and ineffective process even in calm waters.

As for cleaning contaminated animals and birds, the cleaning can often be as lethal as the oil itself because it risks harming the creature's immune system. A 1996 study followed brown pelicans contaminated by oil and tracked the birds that were cleaned and then released into the wild. The majority of the birds died or failed to mate, and scientists concluded that cleaning pelicans could not revive birds to good breeding health.

Cleanups make us feel good because it gives the impression that something is being done. But by and large these billion-dollar projects do not help, and currently there is no truly successful way to clean up a spill.

How Plastic Is Made

Making plastic follows several specific and complicated chemical processes, but essentially it follows four main stages after the fossil fuels have been removed from the ground: refining, cracking, polymerization and production of nurdles.

Fossil Fuels to Plastic

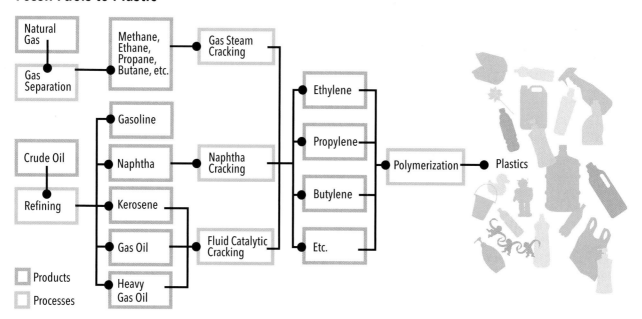

Hydrocarbons are any molecules that are made up of hydrogen and carbon atoms.

Refining

The refining process works differently for gas and oil. Raw natural gas is comprised of a mixture of hydrocarbons (methane, ethane, propane, butane, pentanes), water vapor and other compounds (hydrogen sulfide, carbon dioxide, helium, nitrogen, etc.). Complex processes remove water and impurities, eventually resulting in purified natural gas liquids (NGLs), like ethane, the most important natural gas product involved in plastic production.

When it comes to oil, the crude extracted from the ground is a soup of different hydrocarbons. Crude oil on its own isn't particularly useful until refined into other products. Refining converts crude into petroleum products like gasoline, diesel, jet fuel and naphtha (a flammable liquid mainly used to dilute crude oil and as a fuel). For this to happen crude oil is heated and broken down into different layers known as "fractions." These fractions are separated by their weight and boiling point, with heavier fractions falling to the bottom and lighter fractions rising to the top. The most useful fractions for making plastic are naphtha, kerosene, gas oil and heavy gas oil.

Cracking

Cracking, like the name suggests, is the process of taking long chains of hydrocarbons and breaking them apart into smaller molecules, or monomers. The word "monomer" comes from the ancient Greek root words "mono," which means one, and "mer," which means part.

Different methods of cracking are used depending on the fuel. For example, a natural gas like ethane is broken apart with a gas steam cracker, naphtha with a naphtha steam cracker and kerosene, gas oil and heavy gas oil with a process called fluid catalytic cracking. For each of these processes you need high pressure and high temperature. In steam cracking, liquid hydrocarbons like ethane and naphtha are diluted with steam and quickly heated in a furnace. The cracking temperature plus the time in the furnace determine the resulting molecules. Naphtha can produce ethylene, propylene or butylene depending on the methods. Fluid catalytic cracking requires not only heat but also a solid acid catalyst for the reaction to take place. A catalyst is a substance that enables a chemical reaction to take place either faster or under specific conditions.

The resulting products, such as ethylene, propylene and butylene, are referred to as petrochemicals. Petrochemicals are used to make plastics, but they also can be used to create many other products, including adhesives, paper products, inks and pharmaceuticals.

Polymerization

In the next stage, petrochemicals undergo polymerization. Polymerization is the process of taking monomers and turning them into polymers (polymer means "many parts"). This is done by reacting monomers together to form polymer chains using specific temperatures and a catalyst. For example, ethylene (C_2H_4) is a molecule made of two carbon atoms connected by a double bond. The reaction of multiple ethylene molecules in the presence of a catalyst breaks the double bond and connects the carbon atoms in a long polymer chain, which creates

In the United States alone there are:
- 135 petroleum refineries
- 510 active natural gas processing plants
- 29 ethylene cracking plants

Polymerization of Ethylene

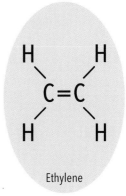

Ethylene

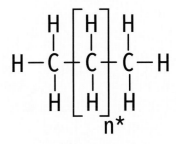

Polyethylene

* "n" means structure in brackets repeats "n" number of times.

So Long, Polybutylene

Sometimes, like fashion, certain types of plastic go out of style. Polybutylene was once commonly used for pipes in millions of homes. But this quickly stopped, and for good reason. The pipes would often leak or break down when in the presence of chlorine, which is commonly used to treat drinking water in many municipalities. These leaky pipes were even subject to a class-action lawsuit, *Cox v. Shell Oil*, which was settled for $1 billion in 1995.

Nurdles typically range in size from 1 to 5 millimeters (0.04 to 0.19 inches).

polyethylene. Similarly, a catalyst can convert propylene into polypropylene and butylene into polybutylene. Different monomers combined with different catalysts are being tested frequently to create new types of polymers.

The refining, cracking and polymerization processes will sometimes take place within the same factory compound; other times the ingredients are shipped throughout the world, and each phase is completed independently.

Nurdles

The polymerized liquid is cooled and then chopped into tiny pieces called nurdles. A single nurdle is no bigger than a pea, and barrels of these tiny pieces of plastic are shipped around the world to make millions of different plastic items.

Production on the Rise

The demand for fossil fuel for energy and transport has been shrinking. As many of us move to electric vehicles and more fuel-efficient combustion engines, less oil is required. But oil companies are not overly concerned because despite mounting public concern over plastic pollution, plastic production is growing rapidly and is expected to continue rising. According to the International Energy Agency, the world's energy watchdog, demand for petrochemicals will offset the slowing oil demand for transport by 2050.

In 2017 global demand for petrochemicals accounted for roughly 12 million barrels a day. But by 2050 that number is expected to balloon to 18 million barrels per day. From this, the World Economic Forum anticipates that plastic production will grow 3.8 percent every year to 2030. Many experts attribute this accelerated growth to the rise

in cheap shale gas from fracking in the United States. The shale gas boom has led to the dramatic increase of new infrastructure to produce plastic. For example, in September 2018 the American Chemistry Council reported investments of over $200 billion on 330 new or expanded facilities.

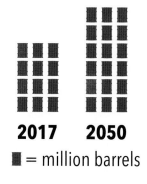

2017   2050

■ = million barrels

Markets for plastic and plastic products are expected to grow especially in Asia and the Middle East. Of course, these are only estimates and consumer protest can influence these projections, but the link between plastic and fossil fuels is undeniable. To truly fight plastic pollution, changes need to occur within the fossil fuel economy.

Types of Plastic

How do you turn tiny plastic pellets into the plastic products we use every day? Step one is to turn up the heat. Manufacturers heat nurdles until they are about the consistency of modeling clay. In a process called plastic extrustion, machines inject the hot plastic into molds of whatever shape is needed. While in the mold the plastic hardens, and a machine then pushes the plastic shape out of the mold. This process can happen rapidly, and when multiple molds are used a lot of plastic products can be made. This is one of the reasons plastic is such a popular material; it can be molded into almost any shape and quickly.

If you are curious about what type of plastic was used to make, say, your shampoo bottle, check for the "Resin Identification Code." For example, if you see the symbol ⚠, the "5" stands for polypropylene (PP). In America, six plastics (PET, HDPE, PVC, LDPE, PP, PS) all have a unique resin code. The remaining plastics are categorized as No. 7 "Other" (O).

Plastic Extrusion Process

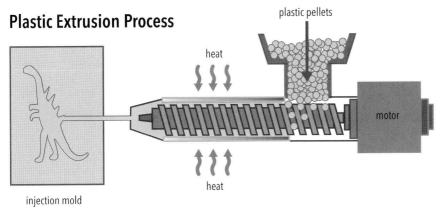

injection mold

For plastic textiles the process has a few more steps. The base plastic for most polyester is polyethylene terephthalate (PET). This plastic base is melted to form a syrup-like solution and then directed into a metal container called a "spinneret," which forces the plastic through tiny holes. The number of holes determines the size of the yarn as the extruded fibers are brought together to form a single strand. At this spinning stage other chemicals might be added, such as flame retardant. As the extruded fibers are drawn they are wound on large bobbins ready to be woven into material. This process is called melt spinning.

Melt Spinning Process

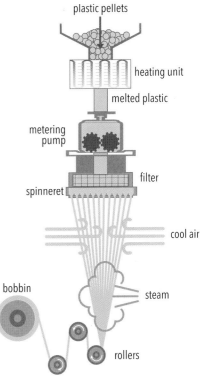

The term plastic covers many unique types of material. There are hundreds of different types of plastic, but according to research conducted in 2015 these are the most commonly produced plastics worldwide:

Polyethylene terephthalate

Abbreviation: PET

Characteristics: Depending on how it is processed, PET can be rigid to semirigid and is a strong and lightweight material. Sixty percent of PET produced is used to make the synthetic fiber polyester.

Examples: Soft drink bottles, textile fibers

Plastic production in 2015: 33 million metric tons

High-density polyethylene

Abbreviation: HDPE

Characteristics: HDPE is an opaque plastic known for its strength. Compared to LDPE it has greater tensile strength (the amount a material can be pulled before it breaks apart) and can withstand greater temperatures.

Examples: Laundry detergent bottles, shampoo bottles

Plastic production in 2015: 52 million metric tons

Polyvinyl chloride

Abbreviation: PVC

Characteristics: You've likely seen a PVC pipe in your home or at a hardware store, and this type of plastic is also used to make bottles, imitation leather, flooring, bank cards and more. Only 40 percent of this plastic is made from petroleum. Like the name suggests, the other 60 percent comes from chlorine, specifically sodium chloride (NaCl), or salt. In the U.S., 10.5 million metric tons of chlorine are produced each year, and about 40 percent of that is used to make PVC.

Examples: Plumbing pipes, medical supplies (e.g., blood bags)

Plastic production in 2015: 38 million metric tons

Low-density polyethylene

Abbreviation: LDPE

Characteristics: LDPE is a flexible and tough plastic that can be both translucent and opaque. Compared to its sister plastic, HDPE, the molecules that make it are less tightly packed together, making the density lower. This also means it has less tensile strength.

Examples: Plastic wrap/cling wrap used to cover and store food, single-use shopping bags

Plastic production in 2015: 64 million metric tons

♷ Polypropylene

Abbreviation: PP

Characteristics: Polypropylene has many similar characteristics to the polyethylene family, but it is slightly harder and more heat resistant. This plastic is used extensively in packaging.

Examples: Car interiors, toys, plastic packaging

Plastic production in 2015: 68 million metric tons

♸ Polystyrene

Abbreviation: PS

Characteristics: In its original form PS is clear, glassy and brittle, and used for packaging, like cases for CDs (remember those?). But it can also be expanded with air to create foam. Most (95–98 percent) polystyrene foams are made of air, and these are known as good thermal insulators. There are different types of PS foam, but the most common is an extruded polystyrene commonly known as Styrofoam™.

Examples: Refrigerator shelves, CD cases, foam takeout containers, packing peanuts

Plastic production in 2015: 25 million metric tons

♹ Other

Characteristics: This category contains a wide range of different types of plastics and also includes products that are made of more than one type of plastic from categories one to six. Materials grouped as "Other" include polyurethane (PUR), a flexible fiber that that can be used to make stretchy textiles, like spandex; a bioplastic called polylactic acid (PLA); polyamide (PA), which is commonly referred to as nylon; and acrylic, which is made from the polymer polyacrylonitrile (PAN).

Examples: Plastic sponges, building insulation, clothing, furniture, carpets

Thermoplastic vs. Thermosets

Most plastics are "thermoplastics," meaning the polymer can be melted down and reformed. It is this characteristic that allows plastics to be recycled. "Thermosets," on the other hand, cannot be remelted and once formed are "set." Instead, when exposed to heat the material burns and degrades but does not melt. Some examples of thermoset plastics include epoxy, silicone and polyurethane.

Different Plastics, Different Chemicals

As mentioned earlier, 99 percent of all plastic is made from fossil fuels, but for most types of plastic extra ingredients are added in, which vary depending on the type.

Bisphenol A (BPA)

Bisphenol A (BPA) is an additive that makes plastic clear and hard — think of a reusable water bottle. BPA is also used to make the epoxy resins that line metal food containers to keep the contents fresher, like a can of salmon. You might have heard of BPA before because it can easily leach into your body and food. Just by holding a bottle made with BPA you can absorb it into your skin, and this impact is elevated if the bottle has been heated. So if you were to microwave a meal in a container made with BPA, you are more likely to ingest it.

Should you be concerned? Yes and no. Once BPA is in your body it can mimic human hormones. In high enough doses this can disrupt processes in your body that help regulate metabolism, growth, reproduction and sleep. On the other hand, BPA is released from plastic in minute quantities that are unlikely to impact you, though repetitive use could be of concern.

Phthalate

If BPA makes plastic hard, phthalates are added to make plastic soft and flexible. Phthalates are found in plumbing pipes, hospital

What about BPA-Free Plastic?

If you are concerned about the chemical additives in plastic, you might spend time seeking out BPA-free products. But before you spend too much time and money looking for "safer" options, you might want to consider whether the replacement is any better. Some BPA alternatives include BPF, BPS, BPAF or bisphenol 5. Scientists first began to question these replacements during a study that measured the effects of BPA on mice. They had one group of mice drink from a water bottle made with BPA and a second control group drink from one that was BPA-free. They discovered that the control mice experienced similar genetic changes to the ones that drank from the BPA bottle. Both groups had alterations to their chromosomes, which can lead to problems in both egg and sperm production. Of course, these experiments were carried out on mice, so more research is needed to determine if the same holds true for people. But there is evidence that BPA-free products may be too similar in chemical structure to behave any differently.

tubing and even the coating of pills we ingest. It has been linked to birth defects, cancer, diabetes and infertility, but like BPA you would have to come into contact with high amounts of phthalate for it to have a significant impact on your health.

How Much Plastic?

One study calculated that between 1950 and 2015, 8.3 billion metric tons of plastic were created. That's a pretty big number, but how heavy is that really? Consider this: if everyone on Earth stepped on one big scale at the same time, the amount of plastic would outweigh us 26 times over. But what are we using all this plastic for?

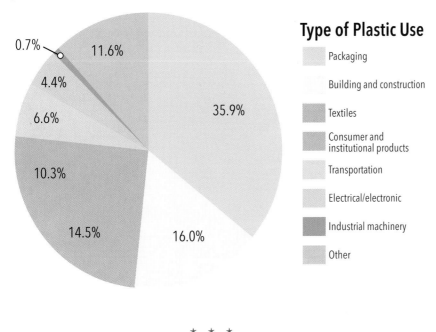

Type of Plastic Use

Packaging

Building and construction

Textiles

Consumer and institutional products

Transportation

Electrical/electronic

Industrial machinery

Other

0.7% 11.6% 4.4% 6.6% 35.9% 10.3% 14.5% 16.0%

★ ★ ★

Plastic plays a role in so many aspects of our day-to-day lives, and in many ways it has changed human culture forever. We are thoroughly surrounded by this "dream material," but what effects has this had on our environment and our health? In the next chapter we explore the environmental impact of plastic — from the highly visible litter to its more inconspicuous effects on our climate.

CHAPTER 2

The Plastic
Problem

As a globe, we produce 190 times more plastic than we did in 1950. We went from producing 2 million metric tons a year to 380 million in 2015. By the end of 2015, an estimated two-thirds of this plastic was discarded as waste, much of it escaping into the land and sea. We're becoming increasingly aware of how plastic waste is damaging Earth's green spaces, rivers and oceans. We can see the litter right in front of us, but plastic also creates pollution that is less visible though just as alarming. This chapter investigates pollution created from not only plastic waste but also plastic production and how all of it contributes to water pollution, air pollution and climate change.

(left) A young boy collects plastic items to use or sell in the Philippines. Plastic waste is a serious issue in the country, which uses over 163 million plastic sachets every day.

Carbon Emissions

As you can see from the graph, when it comes to climate change food waste plays an even greater role than plastic and is one of the biggest environmental crises of our time.

At every point in the life cycle of plastic, carbon dioxide (CO_2) emissions that contribute to climate change are created. One analysis found that in 2015 alone, plastic production and waste emitted 1.7 billion metric tons of CO_2 — 3.8 percent of total carbon emissions that year. That's almost double the emissions from the aviation sector. Basically, if plastic were a country, it would be the fifth-highest emitter in the world.

Highest CO₂ Emitters in 2015

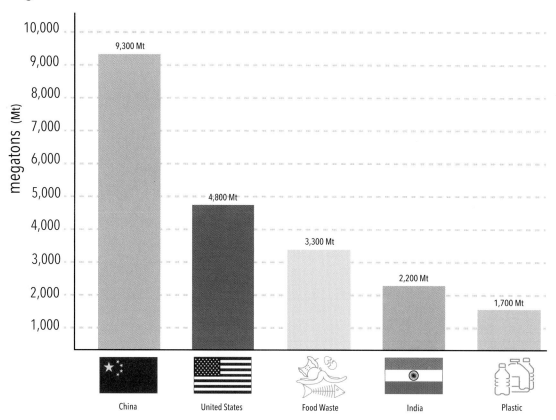

Sources: International Energy Agency; Food and Agriculture Organization of the United Nations; Zheng, J., Suh, S. (2019)

Plastic production is expected to grow, and if it continues at its current rate, by 2050 it could make up 15 percent of total emissions worldwide. This could seriously threaten our carbon budget goals.

Keeping to Our Carbon Budget

A carbon budget is a way to measure the amount of emissions that can enter the atmosphere in order to stay within a global temperature threshold. Since the beginning of the industrial era in the 19th century, Earth's average temperature has risen over 1°C (1.8°F). Through the Paris Agreement, the global community has agreed to limit global warming to 1.5°C (2.7°F) above preindustrial temperatures. This goal has been lowered from the previous threshold of 2°C (3.6°F), but what difference does half a degree really make? According to many scientists' estimates, a lot!

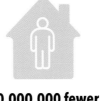

10,000,000 fewer people would lose their homes.

50 percent fewer people would experience water scarcity.

50 percent fewer species would lose their habitats.

However, all agree that keeping within this budget won't be easy, especially if we don't curb our plastic addiction.

Cradle to grave, the life cycle of plastic can be divided into three main sections: production, conversion and end of life.

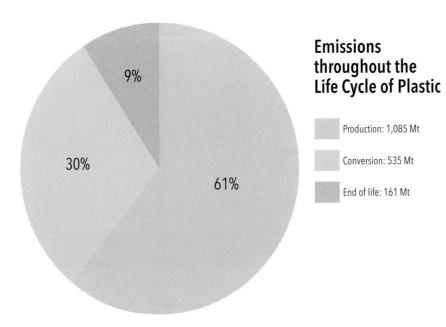

Emissions throughout the Life Cycle of Plastic

Production: 1,085 Mt

Conversion: 535 Mt

End of life: 161 Mt

Plastic Production

Plastic production makes up 61 percent of plastic's greenhouse gas emissions at 1,085 metric megatons (Mt). A significant portion of that comes from the extraction and transportation of the fuels that create plastic. Emissions can come from methane leakage, energy used to drill for oil and gas, and energy used to clear forests and fields for pipelines and oil well pads.

As well, the process to refine fuel and convert it into plastic is both energy and emissions intensive. In the U.S., for example, 24 ethylene plants, which crack ethane into ethylene, generated 17.5 megatons of CO_2 emissions in 2015. That is equivalent to putting 3.8 million cars on the road. Globally, cracking plants emit up to 213 megatons of CO_2 — as much as 45 million cars.

The same study that assessed the life cycle of plastic carbon emissions also assessed how different types of plastic create different levels of CO_2. At the production stage polyester, polyamide and acrylic (which the study called PP&A) have the highest level of emissions, demonstrating the environmental impact of the textile industry. Members of the polyolefin family — including polypropylene (PP), low-density polyethylene (LDPE) and high-density polyethylene (HDPE) — also create significant emissions.

Conversion

During the manufacturing stage of converting raw plastic materials into plastic goods, 535 megatons (30 percent) of CO_2 emissions are produced. Most of this is energy used to power the factories that turn raw plastic into the bags, containers and textiles we use each day. Similar to PP&A's impact during production, PP&A products create the most emissions during conversion.

Metric Ton vs. Megaton vs. Gigaton

Unit of Measurement	Equivalents	How Many Blue Whales?
Metric ton (t)	1,000 kilograms	One blue whale weighs up to 150 metric tons (150,000 kilograms)
Metric megaton (Mt)	1 billion kilograms 1 Mt = 1,000,000 metric tons	Over 6,000 whales
Metric gigaton (Gt)	1 trillion kilograms 1 Gt = 1,000 Mt	Over 6 million whales

Escape of the Nurdles

Plastic litter is something we think happens mostly at the end of the plastic life cycle: we drink from a plastic water bottle and dispose of it, with little concern about where it will end up. But plastic litter can happen at any stage in the life cycle of plastics, and there is no greater evidence of this than nurdles.

Nurdles are tiny pellets of plastic resin that are shipped around the world as raw materials to make numerous plastic goods. No bigger than a lentil and weighing approximately 20 milligrams (0.0007 ounces) each, these tiny pieces of plastic can escape in large quantities. Over 250,000 metric tons make their way into the ocean annually. If you crunch the numbers, that's over 11 trillion nurdles that end up on beaches, floating in the open water and in the bellies of aquatic animals.

These nurdles can end up anywhere. One survey of 32 countries reported nurdle pollution on the beaches of 28 countries. However, their density on shorelines increases depending on wind patterns, ocean currents and whether the shoreline is in close proximity to a production facility. For example, Texas' coastline on the Gulf of Mexico has plastic pollution rates that are 10 times higher than the coastlines of any other Gulf State in the U.S. This makes sense considering that there are 46 companies in Texas that have permits to manufacture plastic materials.

Nurdle pollution is a serious concern because nurdles easily absorb chemicals found in the water. Researchers have found that nurdles are capable of absorbing toxic chemicals, such as DDT, a pesticide that can accumulate in the fatty tissues of animals and is considered a probable human carcinogen; they can also absorb PCB, which is a highly toxic industrial compound, as well as mercury, a neurological and gastrointestinal poison. When marine animals ingest nurdles, the chemicals not only transfer into their systems, but also the pellets themselves can block digestion by filling the animals' stomachs with plastic, which can lead to starvation.

But why would an animal eat plastic? For starters, nurdles look a lot like some fish eggs, a favorite food

This clump of washed-up fish eggs (top) shows why some species might mistake plastic nurdles (bottom) for a food source.

for many aquatic creatures. Plastic can also take on the smell of food; when algae grows on plastic it begins to emit a stinky odor called dimethyl sulfide, which turtles, whales and sharks have learned to associate with food. Studies have found that the more responsive a species is to this chemical smell, the more plastic it is likely to consume.

When it comes to nurdle clean up, there is currently no effective method. Nurdles are often scattered on beaches with organic elements like sand and soil as well as animals that live in the intertidal zone, so trying to remove pellets on a large scale would also mean removing a lot of natural debris. It is also difficult to track who the polluter is as the nurdles can be lost at any point in the production and transportation phases and, because they're so small, can easily be blown by the wind into the environment. Yet even if we knew who was responsible, under the American Clean Water Act manufacturers can legally pollute up to a certain amount. If a company has a permit, it is allowed to release some pollutants into waterways, and this can be equivalent to a significant number of nurdles.

End of Life

What happens to our plastic waste when we throw it away? Two-thirds of all plastic we have ever created has been discarded. Between 1950 and 2015 an estimated 6.3 billion metric tons ended up as waste. So how is all our plastic waste dealt with? Globally, only 9 percent of plastic is recycled (though much more could be) while 12 percent is incinerated, meaning the waste is burned, reducing it to ash, gas and heat. The other 79 percent makes its way to a landfill or escapes into the environment. But how do these waste strategies contribute to CO_2 emissions?

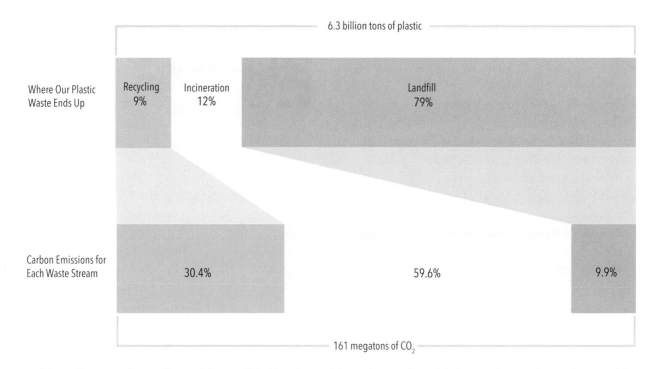

6.3 billion tons of plastic

Where Our Plastic Waste Ends Up

| Recycling 9% | Incineration 12% | Landfill 79% |

Carbon Emissions for Each Waste Stream

| 30.4% | 59.6% | 9.9% |

161 megatons of CO_2

Destroying Earth's Carbon Sink

A carbon sink is a system found in nature that can suck up and store CO_2 emissions, but did you know that the biggest carbon sink on the planet is the ocean? Since the industrial era, the ocean has absorbed 30 to 50 percent of atmospheric CO_2, in large part by the plankton that live there. Phytoplankton have the ability to fix carbon through photosynthesis, but plastic pollution might interrupt this process. Studies are documenting how microplastics are disrupting phytoplankton's ability to absorb carbon and also critically impacting the survival of zooplankton, tiny animals that cycle and export carbon throughout the ocean. So not only is plastic emitting tons of carbon dioxide, but also it is potentially disrupting nature's ability to absorb CO_2, which will have serious effects on our efforts to stop global warming.

Landfills: Low Emissions, Low Impact?

The reason landfills have lower emissions than other strategies is because plastics in landfills take centuries to degrade, so the carbon is more or less locked in. Even biodegradable items like an apple core would take longer to break down in a landfill. The reason for this is oxygen. Substances break down faster in aerobic conditions (with oxygen) because oxygen helps break molecules apart. This process is called oxidation. But most landfills are compacted so tightly that they are anaerobic (without oxygen), and so carbon is locked in for much longer. Incineration breaks plastic down quickly but releases the stored carbon into the atmosphere along with other air pollutants, like dioxins, furans, mercury and polychlorinated biphenyls — all of which have the potential to damage our health and the health of the planet.

As we run out of space to store our waste, incineration becomes a more appealing option, but it is important to weigh the risks it poses. Considering the data on landfill CO_2 emissions it might be easy to assume that landfills are the best waste strategy, but there are many factors to consider. For starters, a lot of waste that makes its way into landfills could be composted or recycled. If everything was just dumped in a landfill, we might run into issues of resource depletion.

A landfill in south-central Florida.

Landfills can also create toxic leachate, a liquid that has passed through solids and gathered chemicals from those solids. When rainwater passes through landfill waste, it can pick up hazardous chemicals from, for example, e-waste or PVC piping and then go on to contaminate groundwater, soil and other water sources. Finally, uncontained landfills allow waste to migrate into the environment, where it causes harm to wildlife.

Cumulatively, the "end of life" phase makes up 9 percent of emissions over the life cycle of plastic — equal to 161 megatons of CO_2. Of the three waste strategies, landfills contribute the least emissions at 16 megatons, with recycling emitting 49 megatons and incineration emitting 96 megatons. This may seem surprising considering that landfills are where the bulk of our waste ends up, and incineration makes up just 12 percent of the waste stream.

For recycling, the 49 megatons of CO_2 calculated does not consider the fact that recycling can reduce new plastic production and the emissions generated by it. If we took this into consideration, recycling emits –67 megatons of CO_2.

Plastic Production and Our Health

Plastic production doesn't just affect the health of the environment, it can also directly affect the health of those who work on the production lines and beyond.

Gases and Dust

In addition to releasing tons of CO_2 into the atmosphere, plastic production and conversion emits several air pollutants, including nitrogen oxide, sulfur oxide and chemical compounds known as volatile organic compounds (VOCs). VOCs react quickly to sunlight and can form smog, which greatly impacts air quality. Smog can worsen existing heart and respiratory conditions as well as irritate the eyes, nose and throat. Many VOC emissions come from the production of polymer foam as well as PVC piping. The plastic and petrochemical industry is also linked to benzene release. Benzene is a human carcinogen that is known to cause anemia and immunosuppression.

Plastic production and conversion also generate a lot of dust, which at high levels can create explosion hazards and pose respiratory risks to those working in a factory.

Workplace Hazards

Making plastic parts can be risky business for workers. A 2013 study that analyzed workers in an automotive plastic factory found that female workers had a 400 percent increased risk of developing breast cancer from plastic fumes versus the general population. Another study found that workers in a plastic factory were more likely to develop respiratory health disorders from airborne particulate.

These plants and factories are disproportionately located in low-income areas, and studies consistently find that industrial air pollution impacts low-income households the most. This pattern occurs on both a local and global scale. In the U.S., which is among the wealthiest nations in the world, polluting industrial facilities are disproportionately located in poor communities. Meanwhile, on the international stage, the most plastic in the world (27.2 percent) is produced in China, which has a significantly lower GDP per capita than the U.S., despite having the world's second-largest economy.

Smoke billows out of a plastic production and processing factory in northern Italy.

Plastic Waste and the Environment

Of all the plastic ever created, two-thirds of it has been thrown away — 6.3 billion metric tons (or 6.3 gigatons). That's a mind-blowing amount of waste that can be difficult to visualize, but it would be equivalent to the mass of 42 million blue whales.

Plastic Waste Generation by Industrial Sector in 2015

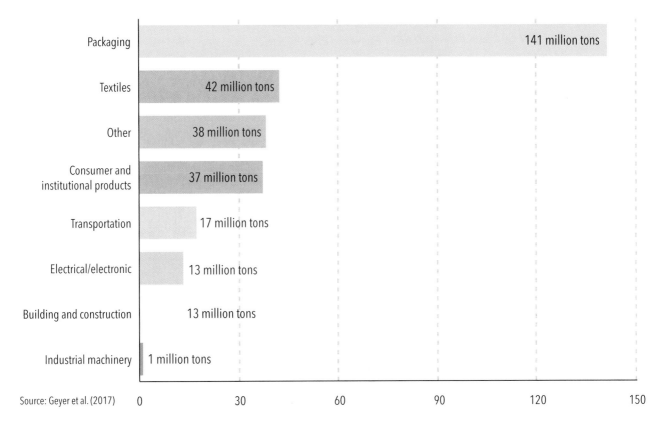

Source: Geyer et al. (2017)

Packaging — 141 million tons
Textiles — 42 million tons
Other — 38 million tons
Consumer and institutional products — 37 million tons
Transportation — 17 million tons
Electrical/electronic — 13 million tons
Building and construction — 13 million tons
Industrial machinery — 1 million tons

0   30   60   90   120   150

The sector that produces the most plastic also produces the most waste: packaging. Over 35 percent of the plastic produced is used for packaging, and in 2015 this sector generated 141 million metric tons of waste.

So much of this waste has escaped capture and disposal. An estimated garbage truck worth of plastic waste enters the ocean every minute. Over the course of a year that equals 8 million metric tons. Approximately 50 percent of this waste comes from rivers taking our trash from deep inland to the open sea.

From Surface to Seabed: Our Plastic Ocean

You can find plastic waste on the shore, surface and seabed of the ocean. But where plastic is found is what influences the impact it has on the environment.

Ocean Surface

Does plastic float? The answer is yes and no. There are a lot of different types of plastic and whether it floats or not depends on density. If it is less dense than seawater — like polyethylene or polypropylene — it will float. Other types have a higher density and will therefore sink, such as styrene and nylon. However, since over half of all plastic is made of either polyethylene (36 percent) or polypropylene (21 percent) most of it does float.

This waste is not spread equally across the surface but congregates in patches across the globe. The largest swath of plastic waste is called the Great Pacific Garbage Patch.

The Great Pacific Garbage Patch

The Great Pacific Garbage Patch is a gyre of marine debris in the north Pacific Ocean. Gyres are formed by a combination of wind patterns, currents, tides, temperatures and salinity — all of which form a circulating vortex of fast-moving water. Gyres are important for circulating water and nutrients but can also pull and trap waste into the center.

When you think of a garbage patch you might think of an island or something you can walk on, but this one's more like a cloudy soup with bits of plastic floating just above and below the surface. Since the patch is not solid it's difficult to estimate its size, but scientists currently estimate it is almost 1.6 million square kilometers (618,000 square miles) — a little less than four times the size of California. There are an estimated 1.8 trillion pieces of plastic trash floating in the patch, and 94 percent of them are microplastics.

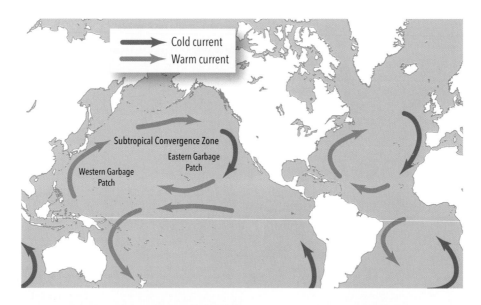

Cold current
Warm current

Subtropical Convergence Zone

Eastern Garbage Patch

Western Garbage Patch

Microplastics: Little in the Middle

Many scientists agree that microplastic (all plastic smaller than 5 millimeters or ⅕ inch) might be the most insidious form of plastic waste, as its tiny size makes it difficult to capture and easy to swallow (thus making its way up the food chain). Finding where in the ocean the bulk of this type of plastic resides is of great importance.

Plastic samples, including many microplastics, collected during the Ocean Cleanup's 2015 expedition to the Great Pacific Garbage Patch.

It was once believed it was all on the surface. Researchers deployed skimmers at varying depths to assess the concentration of microplastics. They observed that at 5 meters (16.4 feet) below the surface the concentration approaches zero. However, a more recent study went a lot deeper and uncovered that microplastic is also accumulating at deep ocean environments (200 to 600 meters or 656 to 1,968 feet below). The concentration here is 12 to 15 particles per cubic meter, which is similar in density to the Great Pacific Garbage Patch. Scientists hypothesize that plastic is finding these depths by hitchhiking through the guts of sea creatures. Therefore, there is a lot of microplastic up top, a lot at the bottom, but very little in the middle.

Seabed

Even plastic that once floated may make its way to the ocean seabed. Why is that? Researchers predict that plastic big and small eventually sinks, weighed down by attached algae or barnacles until its density is greater than seawater. That is why we're finding plastic even at the greatest of depths.

The Mariana Trench is the deepest part of the ocean. To put this into perspective, if you put Mount Everest in the deepest part of the trench the summit would still be 2.1 kilometers (1.3 miles) underwater. Even here, life is consuming plastic. A recent study of amphipods, shrimp-like creatures, found that 70 percent of those living in the trench were eating plastic.

The Beach

We are often bombarded by photos of plastic washed up on the beach, but you might be surprised to discover even some rocks scattered along the beach can be made of plastic. It's true. Rocks made of plastic have been found on Hawaiian beaches. Named "plastiglomerate," these rocks are a mix of plastic, volcanic rock, beach sand, seashells and coral. The rocks are likely formed when plastic melts either through lava flows, forest fires or even campfires.

As for the coastline, some are forming plastic crusts. Along the rocky shores of Madeira, a Portuguese archipelago, researchers

In 2016 scientists discovered what they termed "plasticrusts," a layer of plastic debris, covering the rocky shore of Madeira, Portugal.

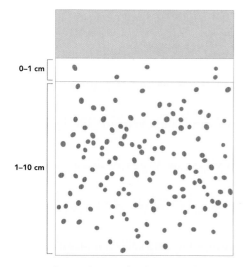

0–1 cm

1–10 cm

Researchers on the Cocos (Keeling) Islands concluded that there is 26 times the amount of plastic buried 1 to 10 centimeters (0.39 to 3.9 inches) under the surface than is visible on the surface.

discovered a layer of plastic encrusted on rocks. The crusts are made from blue and white polyethylene debris that has molded into the rock.

Islands

The Cocos (Keeling) Islands in the middle of the Indian Ocean are extremely remote, and only 600 people live there. Yet a recent study documented 414 million pieces of plastic on its shore, with a total weight of 238 metric tons. This 2019 study shows the layers within the plastic problem, literally. Compared to previous studies that surveyed beach plastic, researchers uncovered a lot more plastic. The reason for this was that researchers dug deeper and discovered 26 times the amount of plastic buried in the sand than was visible on the surface.

Whether plastic waste impacts an island often has little to do with how much waste the island generates and more to do with chance. Where an island is in relation to the gyres greatly influences how much plastic will wind up on its shore, so the plastic litter on an island may have traveled thousands of kilometers to get there. Islands make clear that plastic waste is an international and often borderless issue.

Deadly Debris

As you know, every corner of the planet is touched by plastic pollution — from Arctic ice, to the deepest trenches of the ocean — and wherever it exists, it inevitably touches on the lives of the animals that live there. Though humans are the only animals to make and then waste plastic, it is wildlife, from the tiniest microscopic water flea to the largest megafauna, that bears the burden of our plastic obsession. These are the animals most affected by plastic waste in the environment.

Fish

One often-cited quote is that by 2050 there will be more plastic in the ocean than fish. But how does plastic waste impact fish? One of the primary concerns is ingesting plastic debris. A 2019 study found that 8.6 percent of larval fish (baby fish) sampled were ingesting microplastics. This might sound inconsequential, but larval fish are an enormous source of food for other ocean animals, including sea turtles, sharks and seabirds. From here it is easy to see how plastic makes its way up the food chain.

A larval flying fish (top) and a larval triggerfish (bottom) ingest microplastics, which are zoomed in on the left. A dime is shown on the right for scale.

100 µm

1mm

500 µm

2mm

Ghost Gear

Did you know that fishing equipment makes up 20 percent of ocean waste? An estimated 640,000 to 800,000 metric tons of fishing gear is lost annually. Named "ghost gear," these abandoned nets ensnare countless marine species, severely injuring and killing millions of animals.

Corals

Coral reefs may look like collections of interesting stones and brightly colored plants, but they are actually animals. Plastic can harbor a lot of bacteria, so when plastic waste lands on corals it can make them sick. One particular bacteria, *Vibrio coralliilyticus*, transmits a lethal disease called "white syndrome." Still largely mysterious to scientists, white syndrome leaves white stripes across the coral surface, eventually killing it.

Seabirds

The birds on our planet are having a hard time. An estimated 3 billion birds have been lost in the past half century in America and Canada alone. However, seabirds are declining faster than any other bird group, and plastic in the ocean is one of the chief reasons.

Seabirds are eating a lot of plastic, which can be lethal, but a recent study found that even eating a little plastic can have big consequences. Health concerns include raised cholesterol, lower body weight, impaired kidney function, and shortened wing span and bill length. Sadly, an estimated 90 percent of seabirds have eaten some form of plastic.

A member of the NOAA Marine Debris team disentangles a Laysan albatross chick from a small fishing net in Midway Atoll.

Sea Turtles

Like with seabirds, it doesn't take much plastic to harm a sea turtle. A 2018 study uncovered that just 14 pieces of ingested plastic significantly increases a sea turtle's risk of death. Turtles are prone to eating plastic that resembles their preferred foods. A plastic bag can easily be mistaken as a tasty jellyfish, and a recent study found that green sea turtles were eating plastics that are long, thin and black and green in color — plastics that resemble seagrass, the primary source of food for green sea turtles.

In addition to eating plastic, sea turtles can also get tangled in things such as ghost gear and drown.

Whales

When dead whales wash up on shore, researchers conduct autopsies and examine the contents of their stomachs. The amount of plastic recovered has been staggering. In 2019 a sperm whale stranded in Scotland died with over 100 kilograms (220 pounds) of plastic in its stomach. Another sperm whale, this one pregnant, was found with 23 kilograms (50 pounds) in her stomach. The remains of a squid were also found in her belly, but this food could not provide her body with any nutrients because the plastic waste blocked her digestive system, essentially starving her to death. The same year a 499-kilogram (1,100-pound) Cuvier's beaked whale died of starvation with 40 kilograms (88 pounds) of plastic inside. Tragically, these deaths are becoming the norm.

Seals

Seals can suffer terrible injuries from plastic pollution. It is unclear how many seals globally are impacted by plastic waste, but the records tallied from a single beach paints a sad picture. An animal hospital near a beach in Norfolk, UK, has documented over 51 seals that have required treatment from being injured by plastic waste. And this is just one beach in England, where a small fraction of seals live.

Plastic debris also puts larger mammals, like this endangered Hawaiian monk seal, at risk. Seals can get caught in fishing nets and plastic bags as well as ingest plastic.

Nowhere to Hide

A June 2020 study published in the journal *Science* revealed that there is truly nowhere to hide from our plastic waste. Plastic is in the wind, the rain and the air we breathe. Researchers took 339 samples from 11 national parks and wilderness areas across the U.S. and found tiny particles of plastic in 98 percent of the samples. Plastic accounted for 4 percent of the material found in dust samples. The study estimates that more than 900 metric tons (equivalent to as many as 300 million plastic bottles) of tiny plastic fragments rain down on national parks and wilderness areas in the western United States each year. The impact on human health is unclear; however, previous studies have found that high levels of inhaled plastic is linked to lung disease and tissue damage.

Land Animals

Though research and advocacy primarily focus on marine environments, our waste also impacts land animals. After a 20-year-old elephant was found dead in Periyar, India, an autopsy concluded that the elephant died from internal bleeding and organ failure from eating a considerable amount of plastic waste.

★   ★   ★

The severe environmental challenges of the plastic problem can feel insurmountable, but there are reasons to be hopeful. Though it will take immense effort, with collaboration and commitment from industries, governments, scientists, individuals and innovators, there are accessible changes we can make in our day-to-day lives as well as systemic solutions on the table that are proving effective. In the next chapter we review some of these existing solutions and examine their viability, presenting both the strengths and challenges each solution faces.

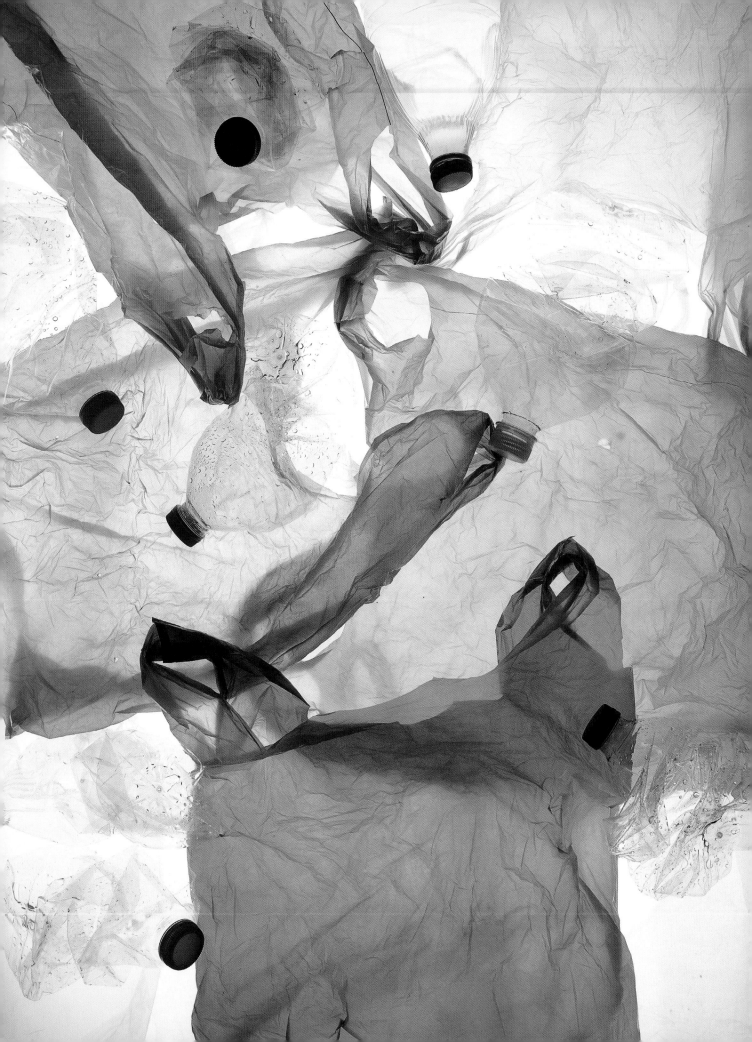

CHAPTER 3

Solving the Plastic Problem

Plastic pollution extends across the globe, from polar ice to the beaches of the most remote islands. Coming up with solutions to such a massive problem is more than a little daunting, but change is possible. This chapter investigates solutions at two scales. Small-scale solutions illustrate how individuals can implement adjustments in their everyday lives. Large-scale solutions feature five ideas that can be implemented at a systems level. Though these ideas have strong potential, they face several challenges; these weaknesses are evaluated critically to help improve the solutions.

Small-Scale Solutions

You've likely heard of the three Rs: Reduce, Reuse and Recycle. But consider adding a few more to your tool belt: Refuse, Repair and Rethink. The following are some practical strategies you can start today to curb the amount of plastic (and nonplastic) waste you generate.

Reduce

There is a reason "Reduce" is at the top of the list for small-scale solutions. Reducing your consumption automatically means a reduction in waste.

Purchasing items locally rather than online means you will support local businesses and avoid the extra packaging used for shipping your items. That bubble wrap and those polystyrene peanuts are all a part of your plastic footprint.

- **Buy less**. One of the biggest changes you can make to reduce waste is simply buying fewer things. Be critical of the purchases you make and take time to really assess if you "need" an item. Impulse shopping not only puts a dent in your wallet (one American survey of 2,000 people found the average consumer makes three impulse purchases a week, adding up to $450 a month), but also this habit eventually takes up space in a landfill. Considering a big purchase? Give yourself 30 days. Write down the item you are thinking of buying and then put it somewhere out of sight. If in 30 days you still want it, see if you can find it secondhand or locally.

- **Borrow from a lending library**. Across the globe, lending libraries of all sorts are popping up, helping people to borrow instead of buy. Tool libraries lend out tools that you might only use one time or very infrequently, like a pressure washer or a saw. Other libraries let you "rent a party," where you can rent items like reusable dishware instead of using single-use plates and cutlery. No lending library? Simply ask friends and family to see if you can borrow the things you need. Borrowing can also be a great test run to see if you really want to invest in buying an item.

Berkeley Public Library's Tool Lending Library offers everything from rakes to cement mixers.

Reuse

A lot of energy, resources and labor go into the items you discard every day. By reusing and selecting items that can be used again and again, you can help ensure that the value of an item is realized.

- **Be prepared**. A little preparation can go a long way. Carry a kit filled with your reusable items. This way it becomes part of your routine. Here's an example kit on the right.

    If you know you need to buy certain items at a bulk food store, clean and pack reusable containers. Many bulk food stores will tare your container before you fill it and subtract the weight of your container when you pay for your goods.
- **Host a free market**. Think of it as a garage sale, except everything is free! Invite your friends to bring items they no longer want, such as clothes, books and housewares.
- **Buy secondhand**. A secondhand purchase can be a less wasteful way to scratch your shopping itch. Also consider this option when purchasing gifts for friends and family.

Refuse

There are items in your day-to-day life that you might accept without thinking about it, but you don't have to. Whether it's refusing a straw for your drink or a free sample from your favorite beauty brand, each refusal can send a message about how you as a consumer are changing your habits.

- **Learn to say "no."** Refusing an item that is offered to us is certainly not easy for everyone. Declining something may be breaking with social or cultural norms and can elicit some discomfort. Here are some tips from trashisfortossers.com on how to refuse a straw. This website is run by Lauren Singer, a zero-waste lifestyle expert who's known for fitting two years' worth of trash into a Mason jar.
    - ◆ Make a request for no straw when you order a drink. It is much easier to ask before you receive a straw than to refuse one when it arrives.
    - ◆ Let people know your intent; one way to do this would be to say, "Could you please hold the straw? I am trying to avoid single-use plastic."
    - ◆ Don't be embarrassed. Feeling confident in your request will often be met with a positive reaction.

Reusable Items to Take with You

Cloth bags for veggies and bread

Container for leftovers

Reusable bag

Set of cutlery

Reusable straw

Reusable cup

Refuse flyers. Consider putting a "No Flyers, Please" sign on your mailbox. In Calgary, Alberta, an environmental organization has distributed over 10,000 of these stickers since 2007, preventing an estimated 1.25 million kilograms (2.75 million pounds) of junk mail. This benefit is twofold: by avoiding flyers you will also be less tempted to buy things you likely don't need. If you love flyers for the deals, you don't have to forgo learning about the weekly specials. Just subscribe to online flyers.

Avoid produce bags. Let's say you are buying six apples from the grocery store. Do you need to use one of the thin single-use plastic produce bags? The answer is no. You can put produce directly into your shopping cart or basket without a bag. Worried about germs from the cart and grocery till? There are absolutely a lot of germs to worry about at a grocery store. But regardless of whether you use a single-use plastic produce bag, there will still be germs on your apples. Consider how many hands have touched your fruits and vegetables on their journey from soil to store. That's why it's essential to wash all your fruits and veggies well. If you need a produce bag for small items like green beans or tender items like grapes, bring your own reusable cloth bags instead. There is no need to purchase these; if you have a T-shirt at home that no longer fits you can convert it into a bag, no sewing required. Search online for "no sew T-shirt bag" for an easy tutorial or follow the instructions below.

> Here's a tip to minimize food waste: wash your produce as you use it, not before you put it away. The moisture from washing speeds up the decomposition rate, spoiling your food more quickly.

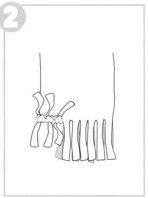

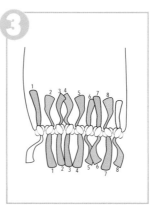

1) Cut off the sleeves of your T-shirt and cut a larger neckline to make your bag handles. Flip the T-shirt inside out and cut vertical strips along the bottom edge of the shirt. You will be tying these strips together to create the bottom of your bag.

2) Tie each pair of strips together snugly, being sure to double knot. Keep one end of the knot above and the other end below, as shown.

3) To close the gaps between the knots, tie the top end of the first knot with the bottom end of the second knot. Next tie the top end of the second knot with the bottom end of the third knot, and so on, until you reach the end. For a neater look, trim the knot ends if you like.

4) Flip the bag right side out, and you're ready to hit the store.

Repair

Learning some basic repair skills can go a long way to extending the life of your belongings and becoming more self-sufficient.

- **Learn a new skill**. Learning how to repair your belongings can greatly minimize waste, save money and foster a new hobby. Perhaps try learning to sew. One of the biggest streams of plastic waste comes from our clothes (see Chapter 4, pages 90–96). A few basic stitches can make your clothes last longer, and there are endless tutorials online. Or even try soldering. A soldering iron is a useful tool for repairing electronics.
- **Find a repair café**. Feeling like you've gotten in over your head? Skilled volunteers are facilitating repair cafés — spaces where you can bring your broken lamp, toaster, jacket, etc. See if there is one in your community. Are you pretty handy? Start one in your community.

Maintaining Your Threads

Think of maintenance as a part of repair prevention. Here are a few tips to keep your clothes looking good longer:

- **Air dry**: Dryers break down your clothing fibers more quickly. Skip the dryer and you'll also save energy and money.
- **Use cold water**: Hot water can cause fabrics, like nylon, to degrade more quickly.
- **Minimize washing**: You can wear an item more than once before washing it. Take your jeans for example: from 2009 to 2010 a student at the University of Alberta wore one pair of jeans for 15 months straight, and he found that they had the same level of bacteria as jeans worn for fewer than two weeks. Though interesting, you do not have to take it to that extreme. A report from Levi's found that its jeans should go 10 wears before hitting the washing machine.
- **Treat stains quickly**: See a stain? Act fast! Read the directions for stain removal products to see if it's appropriate to use on certain fabrics.
- **Wear an apron**: Wearing an apron while cooking can save you from ruining a favorite top or pair of jeans.
- **Zip it up**: The edges of zippers can do a number on other clothes in the wash. So zip up your zippers.
- **Clean off salt**: For those who experience winter weather, salt can be a serious shoe and pant burden. Wiping off salt with a damp cloth and then letting your items air dry before throwing your clothes in the wash can help.

Hire a pro. A hole in your shoe? A broken laptop screen? Even if an item is beyond your repairing capabilities, that doesn't mean you need to replace it. Calling on a professional, such as a shoe cobbler or a computer technician, can greatly extend the life of your goods.

Rethink

Plastic can last hundreds of years and be molded into virtually any shape. Certain types are even stronger than steel. If plastic wasn't so abundant and so cheap to produce, we would perhaps view it as a precious material. Why not flip the script, start rethinking plastic and get creative?

With a little effort and creativity, single-use plastic items like drinking bottles can be given new life as hanging planters.

Make plastic art. Art installations designed entirely from waste are emerging across the globe. But you can also take on a more modest project, such as turning a water bottle into a hanging planter, a homemade toy or a bird feeder.

Buy waste offsets. Have you heard of carbon offsets? Here's an example: when you fly, there is often the option to purchase a carbon offset to compensate for the emissions created during your flight. Scientists and entrepreneurs are proposing using this model for "waste offsets." Depending on the amount of waste you or your business create, you can "offset" that waste by paying an organization to collect waste in a critical area. For instance, your offset could go toward building waste infrastructure in a coastal developing nation.

Vote for science. Voting for candidates who back science and fight for the environment is a way you can address the plastic problem. If such a candidate doesn't exist in your community, consider running yourself.

Recycle

If "Reduce" is at the top of the list because it is the first and most important step in curbing plastic waste, then "Recycle" is at the bottom. As it currently stands it should be the step you rely on the least. Recycling is discussed at length in the following section about large-scale solutions, and though this system faces many challenges, there are several actions that can improve the process.

Large-Scale Solutions

Though the efforts of individuals are an essential part of the plastic problem, these efforts need to be scaled up within communities, corporations and nations to effectively take on the plastic crisis. Though the solutions to this problem are ample and new innovations are continually being discussed, this segment explores five main ideas:

1 Recycling
2 Biodegradable plastic
3 Bans and levies
4 Cleanups
5 Circular economy

Each of these solutions is valuable, but the pitfalls are evaluated as well.

Recycling

When we recycle 1 metric ton of plastic we save 5,238 kilowatt-hours of energy, 16.3 barrels of oil and 23 cubic meters (30 cubic yards) of landfill space. Not only that but recycling feels good. We put our used shampoo bottles in the blue bin and are happy to know that the material will be used to make something new. Unfortunately, this isn't always the case. Recycling is full of potential, but there are several flaws. Worldwide only 9 percent of plastic is recycled, though so much more could be. This section investigates the basics of recycling, its challenges and where changes can be made.

The first curbside recycling program began in Kitchener, Ontario, in 1981. Since then the "Blue Box" has been adopted in over 150 countries.

The PET bottles in these bales have been sorted, tightly compacted and rinsed, and now await recycling.

Recycling 101

Recycling can essentially be broken down into three major steps: collect, sort and process. But along the way this system faces some major roadblocks.

Roadblocks identify challenges in the recycling process.

Collect

Since the late 1990s most curbside blue bin programs have followed a "single-stream" system. This means all recycling — whether paper, metal or plastic — goes into the same bin. Compare this to a multiple-stream system in which waste needs to be sorted. The ease of the single-stream system has caused recycling rates to skyrocket, but it also creates a lot more contamination — so things that don't belong in the bin show up a lot.

Sort

Once recyclables are collected they are brought to a recycling facility. There, a combination of people power and automation sort through the recycling. The mixed waste is loaded onto a conveyor belt and workers begin to pull out items that do not belong, such as plastic bags that could jam the equipment. Waste is sorted through a variety of methods that use gravity, screens and filters. Optical sorting equipment can identify and sort different types of plastic. (Many municipalities do not recycle black plastic because it blends in with the conveyor belt, and the optical sorter cannot identify it.) Sorting is an essential step as contamination can greatly decrease the value of recyclables. From this point sorted waste is often compacted and baled by type and then exported for processing elsewhere, though some facilities do this themselves.

ROADBLOCK
Infrastructure

If you put your blue bin on the curb in front of your home and it was collected, consider yourself lucky. This isn't the case for many. Approximately 2 billion people worldwide are still without regular waste collection. Even in wealthy nations, like the United States, there is an imbalance in waste management. An estimated 34 million rural homes and 16 million apartments do not have access to residential recycling. That's equivalent to 40 percent of American homes. Low population density makes it difficult to afford such infrastructure, which includes trucks that can cost $300,000 each.

ROADBLOCK
Wishcycling

Have you ever held a greasy pizza box or a disposable coffee cup in your hands and wondered, does this go in the recycling? Even if you were unsure you might have just put it in the blue bin and wished that it would get turned into something new. This is known as "wishcycling." In the U.S. 25 percent of everything that ends up in blue bins is not recyclable. This high level of contamination means it's difficult for that recycling to find a market because it is considered lower quality (read about China's National Sword Policy on page 56). If recycling loads are too contaminated, and it's too costly to sort the waste, they will often be sent to a landfill instead.

ROADBLOCK
Dirty Jars

When we toss containers that contain food residue into a blue bin, it can make the recyclables unusable. This is especially true for paper, which is recycled by mixing the paper with water to create a slurry. But oil and fat from food do not mix with water and mingle with the paper pulp, which makes for poor-quality paper. Food residue isn't as big of a deal for plastic, glass and metal as it can be rinsed off. But since most recycling is "single stream," oily jars risk contaminating paper products. The other problem with food waste is sanitation. Food residue can create mold and bacteria that make unsafe conditions for those who work at recycling facilities.

Process

Once sorted and baled, plastic waste can be processed. Magnets and other innovations remove leftover metal and scraps. Plastics are then pre-washed to further remove any debris. The type of plastic determines what kind of "bath" it receives next. For example, a bale of plastic water bottles will be submerged into a hot soapy liquid that removes the labels (the heating process melts the glue that adheres the labels to the bottle). Grinders then shred the plastic into flakes, which are melted, filtered and turned into plastic nurdles. These nurdles are shipped to factories where the plastic can be made into something new.

ROADBLOCK
Low Quality

When we recycle a metal container it can be turned right back into a metal can. The same can be said for a glass bottle. Unfortunately, this is not the case for plastic. Every time a plastic item is recycled, the length of the polymer chain is shortened, which weakens the integrity of the plastic. The degree to which this happens also depends on the type of plastic. Polyethylene terephthalate, for example, is more recyclable than plastic made of polyethylene. Even still, new plastic often needs to be added to improve the strength of the recycled plastic, meaning most recycled goods are not made of 100 percent recycled material. There are many different types of plastic, and when melted together they tend to separate into layers. These blends are not structurally sound and have limited applications. In general, most recycled plastic is "downcycled," meaning it is turned into a lower-grade product than its initial use.

ROADBLOCK
End Market

For those who live in an area with a recycling program, even if you wash your jars and diligently sort your waste, your recycling still might not be recycled. To turn washed, shredded plastic back into nurdles there needs to be someone willing to buy it. You would assume that recycled plastic is less expensive to make than plastic from raw materials, but this is largely contingent on the price of oil. As the price of oil falls, new plastic becomes more appealing and economical to manufacturers — to the detriment of recycled plastic.

China's National Sword Policy

As of January 2018, China has suspended the import of most plastics and other recyclable materials. This ban, named the National Sword Policy, means nearly half of the world's recycling (111 million metric tons) needs to find a new home. You might have assumed that it is your local recycling facility that processes recycled material and then turns it into new goods. For most recycling, however, this isn't the case. Prior to China's ban, the European Union shipped 95 percent and the U.S. 70 percent of their recycled materials to Chinese processors. This "collect-sort-export" model has existed for the past quarter century.

This comes on the heels of international changes in waste collection to a "single stream" system. The bulk of municipalities now place paper, aluminum and plastic all in the same blue bin, whereas in the past consumers were required to sort their recyclables. This change has led to an increase of contamination from food scraps and other unrecyclable garbage that is ending up in blue bins. Adding to the problem is that so much packaging is made of multilayered mixed composites of plastics that contain many colors and additives. This complexity makes it difficult to recycle these materials. Contamination and complexity is one of the chief reasons for China's ban. It now only accepts the cleanest and highest grade materials with 99.5 percent purity — standards most nations cannot meet with the current infrastructure.

The repercussions of the ban are already being felt throughout the world. In Australia 1.3 million metric tons of recyclables previously sent to China now sit in stockpiles. The UK has dramatically increased its incineration rates. In 2018, it burned 11 million metric tons of waste — up 665,000 tons from 2017. In the U.S. the rising costs of operations for some small towns have caused recycling facilities in several municipalities to shut down entirely.

Though this recycling crisis has created chaos, it also has the potential to create better systems. There is the opportunity for expansion in processing and increased pressure on manufacturers to make their goods more recyclable. The full impacts of the National Sword Policy are not yet known, but it certainly has sparked a conversation about how the world deals with its waste.

Recycling in Norway

In Norway 97 percent of all plastic bottles are now recycled. This goal was achieved through the efforts of both consumers and producers. Consumers are charged a levy on all plastic bottles they purchase, but they are able to recoup the expense by returning the bottles in "reverse vending machines" (you deposit the bottle and the machine gives you money back). Meanwhile, producers of plastic bottles are taxed substantially, but if nationwide recycling is higher than 95 percent, the tax is waived. This incentivizes producers to make bottles that are easily recyclable.

Recycling Sleuth: Where Does Your Recycling Really Go?

When we drop an item in the recycling bin, we assume it's going to be recycled. But is this always the case? Undercover reporting by the Canadian Broadcasting Corporation (CBC) investigated this question by purchasing 9 metric tons of plastic. The type was "film plastic," which was mostly shopping bags that had already been sorted and compacted. Using an alias, the CBC hired three different major waste collection companies to recycle the material. GPS trackers were inserted into the bales by the organization Basel Action Network, a nonprofit that fights the exports of hazardous waste from high-income nations to low-income nations and specializes in tracking waste. The trackers work by pinging their geographical coordinates every two to three minutes. Of the nine trackers installed, three trackers malfunctioned; luckily at least two from each company remained intact.

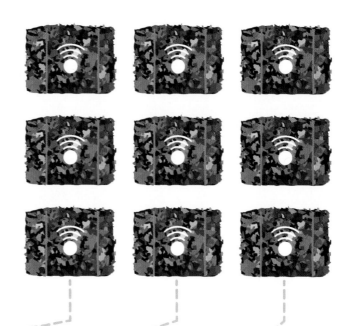

The tracked bales sent to Company 1 (Merlin Plastics) made it to a recycling processing plant. The company later confirmed that the bales were shredded, washed, turned into nurdles and then sold to a customer to make similar material.

The plastic sent to Company 2 (Green For Life) went directly to a waste-to-energy plant that creates power by incinerating waste. (For more information on the concerns around incineration, go to Chapter 2, pages 34–35.) When asked about the decision the company claimed that conventional recycling would have been the preferred solution, but there was no customer willing to purchase the processed plastic.

Company 3 (Waste Connections) stated that the plastic would be sent to a recycling facility, but instead it went directly to a landfill. The company did not respond to the CBC for comment.

In Canada, these companies are contractually obligated to recycle curbside plastic (though this is not the legislative requirement everywhere in the world, including in parts of the United States). However, the companies have no obligation to recycle waste collected from industrial, commercial or institutional sectors. This certainly can feel disappointing. Recommendations on how this can be remedied are discussed on pages 58–59.

Recycling Revamped

As you can see, recycling has its issues. With modification, however, recycling can be a useful tool in mitigating our plastic problem. The following investigates ways in which we can make the process better at each stage.

Design

Before an item ends up in a blue bin — and even before it ends up in your shopping cart — manufacturers can improve recycling by making products easier to recycle. For example, products made of uniform materials can help increase recyclability.

When selecting packaging, manufacturers could consider recyclability and limit the use of unrecyclable material. This could be incentivized by legislation or even global agreements. Over 400 companies and organizations have signed on to the New Plastics Economy Global Commitment led by the Ellen MacArthur Foundation in collaboration with the UN Environment Programme. One of the goals of this commitment is for all packaging to be 100 percent reusable, recyclable or compostable. Though these companies — which collectively make up 20 percent of all plastic packaging globally — have signed the commitment, they each have different timelines of when they will reach that goal.

One particular challenge to recycling is that there are currently over 30 different types of plastic used for packaging. Innovators are working toward creating a "super plastic," one that could fit every form and function required. Though it hasn't been developed yet, such a plastic that meets multiple performance needs could significantly amplify recycling rates.

Collection

Changes in policy have proven to increase the amount of recycling. In the U.S., states that have incentives for bottle collection

A plastic punnet of grapes is displayed next to a cardboard one designed by global packaging company DS Smith. In 2019 DS Smith announced a partnership with the Ellen MacArthur Foundation to create packaging designs for a circular economy.

have higher recycling rates. In Oregon, where there is a "bottle bill," or legislation that mandates that bottles can be returned for a refund value, 90 percent of beverage containers are recycled, more than triple the national average (29 percent).

As discussed on page 57, recycling companies rarely have an obligation to recycle commercial, industrial and institutional waste. Regulations placed on these private industries could significantly impact corporate accountability.

Sorting

So much of the recycling process is out of an individual's control. But you can do your part by making sure your recycling is clean and acquainting yourself with your municipality's guidelines on what is and isn't recyclable. On a larger scale, municipalities may consider investing in ad campaigns about not only what waste belongs where but also what that waste will become. A 2019 study found that when consumers were told what their waste would be transformed into, they were more likely to recycle.

An alternative sorting solution is to return to an older system. Communities with high contamination rates may find greater success with a multiple-stream system (paper, metal and plastic sorted separately), because it would push residents to be more mindful of what goes in the blue bin. A single-stream system can lead to more wishcycling and non-approved items in the bin.

Processing

By and large, processing recycling is done by mechanical methods: shredding, melting and then reshaping into nurdles. As we know, this process changes the properties and degrades the quality of plastic polymers. But scientists are beginning to uncover alternative methods of reprocessing materials so that they are good as new. Chemical recycling breaks down plastic into its original building blocks. This strategy could mean plastics could be recycled an infinite number of times without losing quality. A factory in Kawasaki, Japan, has implemented gasification, a type of chemical recycling that converts plastic into synthesis gases (made up largely of hydrogen and carbon monoxide), and is able to process over 63,000 metric tons of plastic annually.

Locals in Taipei sort their recyclables in trucks that circulate twice a day. Once called "Garbage Island," Taiwan has transformed into one of the world's most efficient recycling nations because of its rigorous recycling program.

Biodegradable Plastic

There are two main categories for conventional plastic alternatives: bioplastics and biodegradable plastics. They sound the same but are quite different.

Bioplastics are produced from renewable biomass sources, in other words anything that was once living. This includes plant matter and sometimes animal extracts. The most common type of bioplastic is polylactic acid (PLA), which is derived from sugars found in corn starch, cassava or sugarcane. How do you turn corn kernels into plastic? The kernels are ground and then the oil is removed from the starch. Starch is made of long chains of molecules. Citric acid is added as a catalyst to stitch the starch molecules together, forming long chain polymers. PLA exists in many forms and can be used to make film, bottles, foam, cutlery, textiles and auto parts.

Biodegradable plastics are plastics that can be decomposed by the actions of living organisms, usually microbes, into basic compounds: water, carbon dioxide and biomass.

These products are sometimes made from bioplastic, but more often they are made from fossil fuels. What makes them different from conventional plastic is that additives are put in to make it biodegrade.

To review, most bioplastic is biodegradable, though some is not. Some biodegradable plastic is made from bioplastics, though most is not.

Does It Degrade? Not Necessarily

An item might be labeled as biodegradable, but how do we know that is true? If we left it on our window ledge, would it turn to dust in a matter of weeks? To find out, scientists from the University of Plymouth in the UK conducted a series of experiments (a bit more rigorous than the window ledge test). They tested two conditions: first they buried both biodegradable bags and conventional plastic bags in soil for three years; second they submerged the same two types of plastic bags underwater for three years. The results? In both conditions, the biodegradable bag and conventional plastic bag each maintained its shape and even its strength. After even three years of being buried in soil or submerged in water, the biodegradable bags could still hold the weight of a 2-kilogram (4.4-pound) load of shopping without tearing. This isn't what most consumers would expect when they

Plastic, even biodegradable plastics, might never *perfectly* degrade, but there is potential to convert plastics into something new. Scientists have devised a chemical recycling process that takes some types of plastic waste, such as polyethylene and polypropylene, and converts it into the fuel naphtha.

Plastic-Eating Bacteria

A defining characteristic of most plastics is that they will not biodegrade. But in 2016 a rare bacteria called *Ideonella sakaiensis* was discovered — and it eats plastic! Scientists are working quickly to see if these microbes could work at scale. Currently, a colony can degrade one PET bottle in a few weeks to months. That's way faster than the hundreds of years it would take for the bottle to degrade unassisted, but it's not quick enough to use in an industrial-scale device that digests plastic, for example. One strategy is to use adaptive laboratory evolution. By observing which bacteria are best at digesting plastic, the best plastic eaters are picked for the next generation of cultivation.

Another promising approach involves an enzyme that has been shown to degrade 1 metric ton of plastic bottles up to 90 percent within 10 hours. What remains is the chemical building blocks to create new food-grade plastic. This discovery was published in April 2020, and researchers are already partnering with members of the food and beauty industries, such as PepsiCo and L'Oréal.

Despite these possibilities, experts caution that there are risks involved. If plastic-eating microbes escaped the laboratory they could begin to degrade our world that is made in so many ways of plastic.

see something labeled biodegradable. However, many plastic alternatives need a certain suite of conditions to decompose, which is explained later.

Where Does the Waste Go?

With terms like biodegradable, compostable and bioplastics, it can be difficult to determine which bin to put this waste in. Does biodegradable plastic belong in the compost bin or the recycling bin? Or is it actually supposed to go to the landfill?

The confusion can be linked to three factors: first, municipalities vary in their capacity for dealing with these materials; second, biodegradable plastics and bioplastics are not uniform but made of varying ingredients; and third, instructions on packaging are nonexistent or, at best, unclear. For example, food vendors at a music festival in Sweden served dishes on cornstarch-based plates. Festivalgoers assumed these plates would break down in nature (like an apple core), and so they just littered them on the ground instead of putting them in a compost bin.

It's true that some bioplastic and biodegradable plastics could decompose if left on the ground or put in a home composter, but most (like those cornstarch plates) require certain conditions, such as those found in industrial composters, to biodegrade. The plastics may also need prolonged exposure to temperatures of 57°C (135°F) or higher. As you can imagine, if plastic escapes into the ocean and requires these types of conditions to degrade, they simply will not break down. If littered in the environment, these plastic alternatives pose the same risks to ecosystems and animals as conventional plastic.

Though an influx of alternative materials are being used to create plastics, 99 percent are still made from fossil fuels. With this in mind, municipalities may not view investing in the appropriate infrastructure as a warranted expense. This is a real chicken-and-egg scenario — more bioplastics will be created if there are ways to manage the waste, but waste facilities won't be created until there are more bioplastics. Until these facilities exist in our communities, the appropriate place to put this kind of waste is, unfortunately, in the garbage.

New Materials

The bioplastics available today at a mass scale certainly have their imperfections, but this doesn't mean we should stop trying to find better materials. Here are some creative plastic packaging alternatives:

- **Shrilk**. A product of a Harvard University lab, Shrilk is a clear, inexpensive plastic engineered from both chitosan, a structural element found in the exoskeleton of shrimp, and a protein from silk, which is derived from insects. This material has the potential to be used for flexible film and rigid shapes.
- **Mycelium**. Mushrooms are amazing organisms that have an intricate network of roots called mycelium, and these roots are being used to make packaging in a fascinating way. The company Ecovative first collects agricultural waste and wood chips as a growth medium to cultivate mycelium. The mycelium then breaks down the waste and wood chips, coating them in its white root matrix. The mycelium-coated fragments are then placed into different molds depending on the desired packaging. Within a few days the mycelium grows into a solid structure that takes the form of the mold. The mycelium packaging is then dried to stop the growing process. It's comparable in appearance to extruded polystyrene This creates a nontoxic and compostable packaging material that can grow into myriad shapes.
- **Water bites**. Imagine biting into a drink of water. A package-free water ball, made by the start-up Skipping Rocks Lab, is

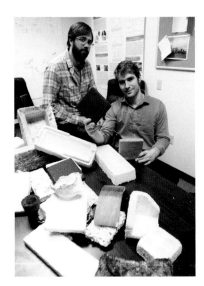

Ecovative co-founders, Gavin McIntyre (left) and Eben Bayer (right), pose with some of their mycelium products.

equivalent to a few swigs of water. It's made by taking balls of ice and dipping them into plant and seaweed extracts (a material the company calls Notpla), which form an edible membrane around the water. You pop the water ball in your mouth, take a bite, swallow the water and then swallow the plant-based membrane, too. If these water bites were handed out at races, they could keep 2.3 million cups off the road just for the New York City Marathon. The company also produces compostable condiment sachets made of the same material.

Bans and Levies

Out of 192 countries reviewed, nearly two-thirds (127) have adopted some form of national legislation around single-use plastic bags. This includes total bans, partial bans, levies and more. Here are some examples from around the globe:

One of the biggest barriers to adopting package-free food is adjusting human psychology and behavior. For example, edible packaging called WikiCells was made to envelop single servings of package-free frozen yogurt, but consumers found grabbing an unwrapped product unappealing and the product failed.

America does not have any federal regulations, but there are some bans at the municipal and state levels, including eight states: California, Connecticut, Delaware, Hawaii, Maine, New York, Oregon and Vermont. However, 14 states have regulations that actually ban plastic bag bans.

In Norway the onus to deal with plastic falls on the producer. If a producer puts packaging, such as a plastic bag, into the market, it is responsible for funding the collection, sorting and recycling of the used packaging.

Norway

Ireland
See page 64

United States

Antigua and Barbuda

Costa Rica
See page 65

South Africa
See pages 64–65

Madagascar

Fiji

In Antigua and Barbuda, it is prohibited to import, distribute, sell or use plastic shopping bags, and a breach of these rules can lead to a $10,000 fine and imprisonment of up to one year. There are exemptions for specific bags, including those for agricultural uses and sanitation or waste storage.

Thirty-eight countries regulate the thickness of plastic bags. The reason being thin bags are more likely to jam waste management machinery and also escape into the natural environment. Madagascar, for example, doesn't allow any bags thinner than 50 microns – approximately half the thickness of a standard piece of paper.

In Fiji, there is a levy of 10 cents per plastic bag.

A road in Dublin, Ireland, is littered with plastic bags and other pieces of garbage.

Case Studies from Around the World

The following are three case studies from around the world that deal with bans and levies in different ways. This section reviews the effectiveness of these strategies.

Ireland: Levies on Consumers

In the 1990s plastic bag litter was a big problem in Ireland. The average resident was using 328 bags per year, and bags alone made up 5 percent of the waste stream. In 1998 Ireland's Department of the Environment, Heritage and Local Government commissioned a study to see what citizens were willing to pay for a bag. The amount was 0.024 euros ($0.026). They then multiplied that price by six to get 0.15 euros ($0.16), and by 2002 the levy, dubbed the PlasTax, had launched. The Irish government didn't just release this tax without explanation but created a strong media campaign illustrating the benefits to the environment. This led to strong buy-in and a successful rollout. Within one year Ireland had dropped the number of bags used by 90 percent. Bags only made up 0.22 percent of the waste stream, and only 21 bags were used per person per year.

As time went on, however, bag use began to creep back up, and four years after the implementation of the PlasTax, use was at 31 bags. The government then passed legislation to allow amending the levy each year. With an increase to 0.22 euros ($0.24) consumption fell back to 21 bags. This highlights the importance of monitoring and adjusting strategies as needed.

South Africa: Combined Bans and Levies on Retailers

In the late 1990s plastic litter in South Africa was so bad it was considered the "new national flower." This led to a ban on all single-use plastic bags thinner than 30 microns. Additionally, a levy equivalent to $0.03 was placed on retailers, and the revenues were used to establish Buyisa-e-Bag, a nonprofit that promoted waste minimization and recycling.

The levy on retailers has since grown to roughly $0.08 per bag, but some retailers have reacted by charging consumers between $0.35 to $0.75 per bag. These increases have had the largest repercussions on poorer communities, who use the bags to carry goods over long distances. Initially the levy had some impact, but eventually bag use returned to pre-levy and ban rates. The nonprofit eventually closed, and it was discovered that only 13 percent of the revenue was reaching the organization.

One important lesson learned from this case is to engage the public: consumers and retailers were not informed why the ban was taking place, which lead to low engagement in the program. Checks and balances also need to be in place to ensure legislation is being followed, and the fee needs to be set at a price that motivates changes from retailers, or the cost burden will remain on the consumer.

Costa Rica: Total Single-Use Ban

On World Environment Day 2017, the Costa Rican government announced that by 2021 it would ban all single-use plastic. As of mid-2020, this legislation had yet to be implemented, so the success cannot be fully measured, but the ambition and strategy must be acknowledged. The ban will work to remove not only bags and bottles but also straws, polystyrene containers, plastic cutlery and more. The government is planning to replace all single-use items with ones that biodegrade within six months. Though there are problems with biodegradable plastic (see pages 60–62), the six-month requirement is a strong intervention.

Driftwood intermingles with plastic waste on Nancite Beach in Santa Rosa National Park, Costa Rica.

Ways to Improve Bans and Levies

As you can see, there are a lot of bans and levies throughout the world. So then why do we still have so much plastic waste? The following are ways in which we can improve these waste management strategies.

- **Regulate plastic throughout its life cycle**. Though there are several bans on the retail of plastic bags, legislation is lacking when it comes to the life cycle of plastic. In China, imports of plastic bags are banned, and consumers are charged a levy, but plastic bags are still produced and exported. For bans to work it is necessary to regulate the manufacturing, use, distribution, trade and disposal of plastic bags.
- **Evaluate partial bans versus full bans**. Most nations opt for partial bans instead of full bans, such as in France, Italy and India, where there are no real bans on plastic bags but rather restrictions on thickness. This can lead to several work-arounds by producers.
- **Incentivize single-use alternatives**. Rewarding reusable items with subsidies to consumers may find more success than penalizing consumers for not carrying them. These can often come without expense to the retailers (see the table in Chapter 5 on page 115).

Bans Don't Work for Everyone

For some, alternatives to single-use plastic are not accessible or practical. For example, the flexible bend in plastic straws aid some with drinking, while metal or glass alternatives are choking hazards. Alternatives to plastic are not always more environmentally friendly either. Producing materials like wood and metal has a greater environmental impact in terms of natural resources and CO_2 emissions. Though bans and levies can help shift behavior, it's important to remember this is not a black-and-white issue.

Cleanups

Below are some strategies and innovations to clean up ocean debris and plastic waste. Some critics will argue that investing money and energy in cleanup is fruitless, that focus needs to be placed on "turning off the tap" of waste entering the environment in the first place. Absolutely we need to reduce our volume of consumption, invest in waste management and break up with our plastic obsession. However, an estimated 150 million metric tons already swirls through our marine environments, causing immeasurable damage to wildlife. Cleanup is not the cure, but it is an essential treatment to the disease.

Shoreline Cleanup

For over 30 years the Ocean Conservancy has hosted the International Coastal Cleanup. The cleanup removes trash from beaches and waterways and then documents what was collected. It has spread to over 100 countries and takes place on the third Saturday of September. (Missed the date? Any day is a good day to organize a cleanup in your community.) In 2018 over a million people participated from 122 countries. Below are the top 10 items collected internationally that year:

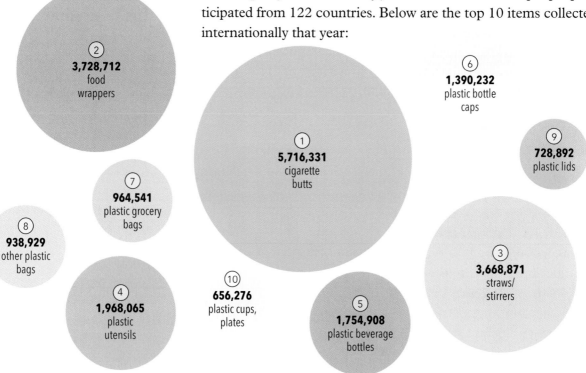

② 3,728,712 food wrappers

⑥ 1,390,232 plastic bottle caps

① 5,716,331 cigarette butts

⑨ 728,892 plastic lids

⑦ 964,541 plastic grocery bags

⑧ 938,929 other plastic bags

③ 3,668,871 straws/ stirrers

④ 1,968,065 plastic utensils

⑩ 656,276 plastic cups, plates

⑤ 1,754,908 plastic beverage bottles

Considering 80 percent of ocean plastic comes from land, picking up litter in your community is a great way to minimize plastic pollution.

Mr. Trash Wheel

The city of Baltimore, Maryland, is home to Mr. Trash Wheel (and the rest of the Trash Wheel family: Professor Trash Wheel, Captain Trash Wheel and a yet-to-be-named fourth member). These 15.2-meter-long (50-feet-long) machines, which are shaped like molluscs, are doing an impressive job of keeping Baltimore's harbor a lot cleaner, which then keeps plastic out of the ocean.

Two booms guide river-borne trash toward a solar- and water-wheel-powered conveyor belt that brings the trash up a ramp, where it is deposited into a dumpster. When the dumpster is full, a boat ships the trash to a waste-to-energy incinerator. In the future, the plan is to be able to sort and recycle the waste instead.

So far, the Trash Wheel family has removed 1,230 metric tons of waste from the harbor. This includes:

- 11,714,398 cigarette butts
- 1,161,782 foam containers
- 1,060,924 plastic bottles
- 701,662 plastic bags
- 4,468 sport balls
- one keg
- one guitar
- one python

Currently there are plans to install Trash Wheels in cities throughout America, including Newport Beach in California, Brunswick in Georgia, and Milwaukee, Wisconsin.

Mr. Trash Wheel was installed in 2014, where the Jones Falls River flows into Baltimore's inner harbor.

Seabins

Think of a Seabin as a garbage can in the water. The bins move up and down with the tides as water is sucked in from the surface, drawing waste into a catch bag inside the bin. Clean water is then pumped back into the marine environment leaving the debris trapped inside. The bins can hold up to 20 kilograms (44 pounds) of waste and have a mesh of 2 millimeters, so they trap microplastics inside, too. The bag can be changed multiple times a day if needed. Worldwide there are now 860 Seabins that capture 3,612.8 kilograms (7,964.9 pounds) of waste a day. At the time of writing, they've kept over 800,000 kilograms (1,763,698 pounds) of debris out of our waterways.

The Ocean Cleanup's System 001/B is seen in the Pacific Ocean as it tests a method of retaining as much plastic as possible.

The Ocean Cleanup

The Ocean Cleanup is an organization dedicated to an ambitious cleanup project with an aim of removing 90 percent of ocean plastic. Beginning where the largest density of ocean plastic exists, the Great Pacific Garbage Patch, the organization set up a giant, flexible tube that floats on the water with a large screen that hangs from the tube below the surface of the water. Currents push the device throughout the patch as it corrals

Ending Ghost Gear

Ghost gear and ghost fishing are terms assigned to abandoned fishing nets that continue to trap and kill fish and other marine life. An estimated 800,000 metric tons of these nets have been lost during storms or become entangled on corals or fishing traps left on the ocean floor. The strong plastic fibers used to make these nets means one net can cause centuries worth of damage. Potential solutions to this problem include creating incentives for fishing companies or individuals to report lost gear, establishing collection facilities at ports where old gear can easily be disposed of and attaching GPS trackers to gear to mark the location where nets were lost, so they have a better chance of being recovered.

Who's to Blame for Litter?

We can all agree that litter is a bad thing, but did you know that anti-litter campaigns might not have the most innocent of origins? The 1950s saw a meteoric rise in consumerism in part from the ease and affordability of plastic, but this increase also meant a lot more pollution. With public pressure, legislatures began to consider regulations that would require manufacturers, especially the packaging industry, to be held accountable and make less junk in the first place.

These changes could have had a drastic impact on profits, but packaging companies lobbied hard against these policies. As a means to shift responsibility and clean up their images, product industry leaders, including Coca Cola and the Dixie Cup Company, came together to devise a plan. The result was "Keep America Beautiful," a massive media campaign that targeted bad environmental practices — but of individuals not businesses.

IN THE FIGHT AGAINST LITTER AND POLLUTION, WE STILL HAVE SO FAR TO GO.

The "Keep America Beautiful" campaign featured the "Crying Indian" Iron Eyes Cody — played by a non-Native American actor — famously shedding a single tear in response to a polluted landscape.

This campaign essentially flipped the script and steered the blame toward individual litterbugs as the main culprits of the garbage problem. This campaign worked in favor of manufacturers. Today there are several anti-littering laws for individuals across America, but there are minimal laws that regulate the packaging industry.

garbage. The floating tube traps large plastic waste on the surface while the skirt traps smaller particles floating underwater.

Though its beginnings were rocky — there were several failed attempts — the device successfully started collecting plastic as of October 2019.

There are several criticisms of the Ocean Cleanup project, including how the device can potentially imperil marine animals. Continual monitoring and modification when needed is necessary for the project to be a success.

Circular Economy

Ninety-one percent of the world's economy is linear, meaning most goods pursue a straight line following a "take-make-waste" model. We "take" resources such as fossil fuel, we "make" plastic products and then we discard them as "waste" to the landfill. This model is often considered the easiest and cheapest, but it relies on two false assumptions:

1 Resources are unlimited.
2 There is unlimited room for waste.

There is an alternative, and it's called a circular economy. This model relies heavily on the 6 Rs, but is scaled beyond an individual level. The following are examples of a circular economy in action.

Garment Hangers

Braiform is one of the largest garment hanger suppliers in the world, but unlike other companies 80 percent of its goods (hangers) are reused. In 2014, 540 million hangers were collected from retailers; of those, 430 million were reused. The ones that were in too poor of a condition for reuse were shredded to make new hangers, so 30 million hangers were made from their own waste stream.

Loop deliveries are made in a durable Loop tote to cut down on single-use packing materials, such as cardboard boxes, Bubble Wrap and ice packs.

The "Milkman Model"

A new company called Loop has partnered with several brands to bring back the "milkman" model. Instead of going to the store to buy, say, a carton of ice cream that will be thrown away when finished, Loop will deliver ice cream in a reusable container directly to the consumer. When the container is empty, it is picked up from the consumer's home, washed and then refilled. Loop is proposing this same system for a number of products, including shampoo, olive oil and laundry detergent.

Zero Waste Stores

Around the globe, zero waste stores are becoming more common. Customers come with their own clean reusable containers, which are first weighed before they're filled with bulk grains, spices, oils, produce, milk, cosmetics and even meat. Once you form the habit of bringing your own containers it can become a pretty standard shopping trip. Don't have a zero waste store in your town? Ask your local grocery store if you can

still bring your own container for some of your needs. Your deli counter might be willing to put that sliced cheese or meat you want directly into your own container.

Secondhand Goods

Have you ever wanted to purchase something used but were uncertain of the quality and safety? In Scotland, a quality standard accreditation program called Revolve Reuse is being rolled out. This externally validated tool provides businesses with training, a mystery shopper visit and other legislative commitments before they're given accreditation. The intent is businesses that display the "Revolve" standard demonstrate to patrons that they are committed to quality and safety, which could lead to an increase in sales. So far the 30 shops and 20 more that are working on their accreditation have seen improved sales.

★　★　★

As you can see, none of the solutions presented in this chapter is perfect, and there is no one fix to the plastic problem. These solutions need to be applied together, and for anything to be effective they need the engagement of citizens. Explaining policies and practices in ways that clearly show why these changes are meaningful will ultimately lead to better outcomes.

In the next two chapters, we delve deeper into a few of the most common plastic items we use every day, and how we can individually visualize and hopefully reduce our own plastic footprints.

CHAPTER 4

Lifetime-Use Plastic

There are items in our homes and workplaces made of plastic (or partially so) that we may own our entire lives, such as a favorite toy or a car. With increasing frequency, however, we are tossing these items for the newest models instead of repairing them or making do with what we have. This chapter catalogs the plastic items we have with us for longer periods of time.

We also investigate alternative materials and goods as well as habit adjustments related to these plastic items. The merit of the swaps and substitutes is investigated critically. Though some materials may appear more "green" than plastic, this isn't necessarily the case. For example, plastic in cars makes for lighter vehicles and therefore greater fuel efficiency. Many of these alternatives are a valuable means of reducing your plastic footprint, while others might be a case of "greenwashing" and lead to more waste instead.

"Greenwashing" is a term that was first coined in 1986. It describes a marketing technique to make a product appear more environmentally friendly, or "green," than it really is.

What's with the Bottles?

You'll notice that several items in this chapter are represented using empty 2-liter soda bottles. Because so many items in this chapter are only partially made of plastic and the plastic content is expressed in weight, it can be hard to picture what a certain weight of plastic looks like. We've chosen an empty 2-liter plastic bottle — something that most people have interacted with — to help you better conceptualize the mass.

= 40 grams (1.4 ounces)

Swaps and Substitutes Guidelines

No matter what the substitute, consider the following guidelines before switching to a new item.

- **Opt for quality**. An item that is well made and can be used for a long time is often the better option than one of poor quality that will fall apart quickly.
- **Fix it**. Before throwing an item away ask yourself if you or someone else can fix it or even repurpose it into something new.
- **Thrift**. Secondhand shopping can reduce a lot of waste and keep items in circulation instead of in a landfill.
- **Borrow**. Borrowing is a great option for reducing the amount of stuff we consume. Instead of buying a special tool to build a desk or a new dress to attend a wedding, see if a friend can lend you these items.
- **Pause**. Before you make a purchase take a moment to think, "Do I really need this?"

Cars

Cars. They get us from point A to point B and, for some, are an important part of their identity. According to a 2016 census study, there are 1.8 vehicles per household in America, and an analysis by an automotive research firm states, on average, we will each own 9.4 cars in our lifetime.

Since the 1950s, cars have become increasingly more plastic. The average car is now made with 200 kilograms (441 pounds) of plastic. Given the average American car weighs over 1,814 kilograms (4,000 pounds), plastic makes up about 11 percent of the total weight.

The amount of plastic will likely increase, and the added plastic may come from replacing glass with plastic. Currently, polycarbonate (PC) is used for almost every headlight and taillight, and soon it might replace all windows. Some high-end vehicle makers are already substituting steel bodies for ones made of carbon fiber composite. Analysts predict that use of this material will increase 280 percent by 2030.

Spread over a lifetime, the average
person will own **9.4 cars**.

=

That equals **1,880 kilograms (4,145 pounds)**
of plastic, which is equivalent to the weight of
47,000 empty 2-liter bottles.

What Are Carbon Fibers?

Carbon fibers are tiny fibers composed entirely of carbon atoms. They are 5 to 10 microns in diameter — thinner than a human hair. These fibers are very light-weight and extremely strong. They can be blended with plastic to form carbon fiber reinforced polymer, some-times referred to as a "carbon fiber composite." The high strength-to-weight ratio of the carbon fibers makes the polymer an ideal material for aerospace projects. Currently, this material is very expensive to produce, but as technology improves and prices drop, we can antici-pate seeing more of this material in the cars we drive.

A luxury sports car with a carbon fiber bumper.

Comedian and former late-night television host Jay Leno is known for having *a lot* of cars. He has an estimated 181 cars and about 160 motorcycles. Many are classic cars of the pre-plastic era, so it is difficult to estimate the exact amount of plastic in his garage, but it's proba-bly quite a bit.

Why Plastic?

Plastic is cheap to produce, incredibly strong and very light. Its lightness is what makes it most appealing to the auto industry. Lower mass means greater fuel efficiency and, with it, lower greenhouse gas emissions. In fact, lowering the mass of cars by 100 kilograms (220 pounds) can reduce CO_2 emissions by 8 grams/kilometer (0.5 ounces/mile) in cars fueled by gasoline.

Though the goal of plastic use is to reduce weight, it's import-ant to note that cars aren't getting smaller — they're getting bigger. In 1987 cars contained a lot less plastic but weighed an average of 1,461 kilograms (3,221 pounds), which is 353 kilo-grams (779 pounds) fewer than today's average vehicle. Below is a comparison of one of the most popular cars in 1987 versus the most popular vehicle in 2019.

	Ford Escort (1987)	Ford F-Series (2019)
Length	4.3 meters (14.1 feet)	5.3 meters (17.4 feet)
Width	1.7 meters (5.6 feet)	2 meters (6.6 feet)
Height	1.4 meters (4.6 feet)	1.9 meters (6.2 feet)
Weight	1,017 kilograms (2,243 pounds)	1,846 kilograms (4,069 pounds)
Weight/Volume	99.4 kg/m³ (6.2 lb/ft³)	91.7 kg/m³ (5.7 lb/ft³)

Proportionally speaking, plastic has allowed cars to get bigger in size with less increase in mass.

Another reason manufacturers are moving toward plastic is recyclability. In the European Union cars are made with, on average, 16 percent plastic as legislation requires that they can be easily disassembled and that at least 85 percent of the car can be reused or recycled. For this reason, making parts out of thermoplastics that easily melt down into new parts is important.

Where Is the Plastic?

Several different types of plastic may be used in the same car model, but three types make up most (65 percent) of the plastic used in cars:

- 32 percent: polypropylene (PP)
- 17 percent: polyurethane (PUR)
- 16 percent: polyvinyl chloride (PVC)

Below are the plastics used in a typical car:

Types of Plastic Found in Cars:

Acrylonitrile butadiene styrene (ABS)
Acrylonitrile styrene acrylate (ASA)
High-density polyethylene (HDPE)
Polyamide (PA)
Polybutylene terephthalate (PBT)
Polycarbonate (PC)
Polyethylene (PE)
Polyethylene terephthalate (PET)
Polymethyl methacrylate (PMMA)
Polyoxymethylene (POM)
Polyphenylene ether (PPE)
Polypropylene (PP)
Polystyrene (PS)
Polyurethane (PUR)
Polyvinyl chloride (PVC)
Styrene maleic anhydride (SMA)
Unsaturated polyester (UP)

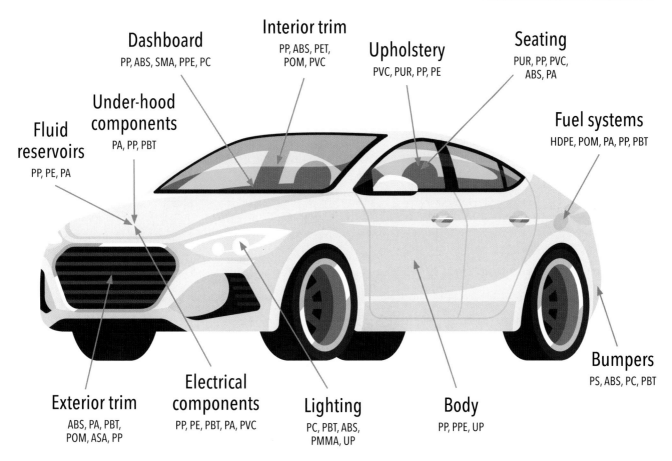

Dashboard
PP, ABS, SMA, PPE, PC

Interior trim
PP, ABS, PET, POM, PVC

Upholstery
PVC, PUR, PP, PE

Seating
PUR, PP, PVC, ABS, PA

Under-hood components
PA, PP, PBT

Fluid reservoirs
PP, PE, PA

Fuel systems
HDPE, POM, PA, PP, PBT

Exterior trim
ABS, PA, PBT, POM, ASA, PP

Electrical components
PP, PE, PBT, PA, PVC

Lighting
PC, PBT, ABS, PMMA, UP

Body
PP, PPE, UP

Bumpers
PS, ABS, PC, PBT

Swaps and Substitutes: Used Cars

Though there are many problems associated with plastic, using this material in cars makes a lot of sense. Unlike single-use items that are used once and then sent to a landfill, cars are used for years and years, and at the end of their lives, parts are often carefully separated and scrap is reused or recycled. However, inventors have fashioned other types of lightweight materials to make cars, which could one day stand as an alternative to plastic.

Ultimately, the best thing you can do to reduce your plastic footprint when it comes to cars is buying fewer. Eventually, you may need to replace your old car, but when? If rust is making the body unsound, if your car is unreliable even after frequent repairs or has been in a serious accident, you should replace your car for the sake of safety. If this isn't the case, consider cruising with the same vehicle for a few more miles. When it is time for an upgrade, think about purchasing a used car.

Electronics

As a planet, we throw away roughly 45 million metric tons of electronic waste, often referred to as "e-waste," each year. That's equivalent to filling over a million large transport trucks. This number is only growing. By 2021 global e-waste is expected to pass 51 million metric tons.

Plastic has become an essential material in making our electronics lighter and smaller, but it makes up only about 17 percent of them by weight.

Recent surveys have found that 96 percent of Americans own a cell phone and 81 percent own smartphones. This has increased 35 percent since 2011. In terms of other electronics, three-quarters of the U.S. population owns either a laptop or desktop, with the majority owning laptops. Half own a tablet and half own an e-reader. Based on popularity this section focuses on laptops and smartphones.

E-waste

Whether we dispose of our electronics because they have broken, or we are just itching for the newest model, most e-waste ends up in the landfill. A United Nations report found that 80 percent of e-waste is disposed of in landfills or incinerators, and that volume is increasing by approximately 40 percent each year. Only 15 to 25 percent of the world's old electronics are recycled or reused. In the United States, e-waste only makes up about 2 percent of the total volume found in a landfill, but this is equivalent to 70 percent of hazardous materials found in a landfill.

Laptops

It's difficult to evaluate the life span of laptops as they are often trashed while they are still operational. On average consumers purchase a new computer every three to five years. Weights also vary considerably with some weighing less than 1 kilogram (2.2 pounds) and others clocking in at nearly 4 kilograms (8.8 pounds). Using the average estimate of four years, if you own your first laptop at age 16 and live to 80, you'll own approximately 16 laptops in your lifetime. If we say the average weight of a laptop is 2.5 kilograms (5.5 pounds), and 17 percent of that weight is made of plastic, each laptop contains 425 grams (15 ounces) of plastic.

Spread over a lifetime, the average person will own **16 laptops**.

=

That equals **6.8 kilograms (14.9 pounds)** of plastic, which is equivalent to the weight of **170 empty 2-liter bottles**.

Where Is the Plastic?

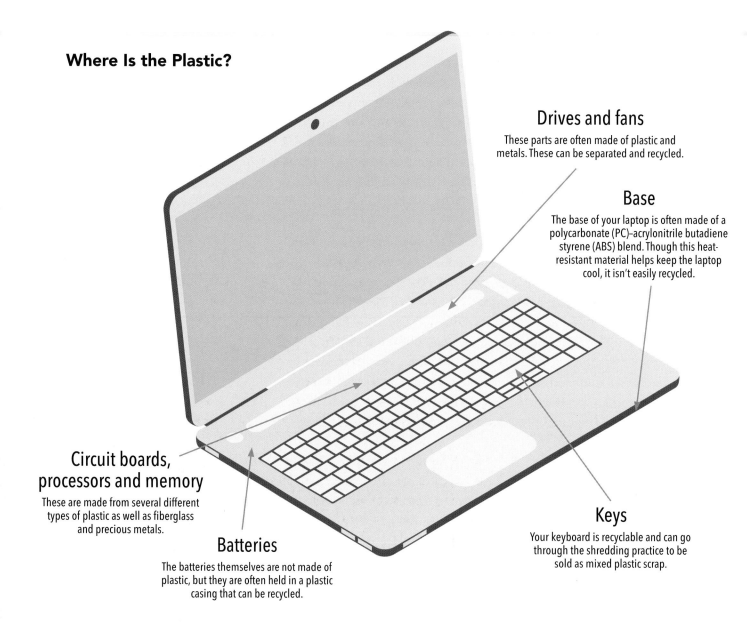

Drives and fans

These parts are often made of plastic and metals. These can be separated and recycled.

Base

The base of your laptop is often made of a polycarbonate (PC)–acrylonitrile butadiene styrene (ABS) blend. Though this heat-resistant material helps keep the laptop cool, it isn't easily recycled.

Circuit boards, processors and memory

These are made from several different types of plastic as well as fiberglass and precious metals.

Batteries

The batteries themselves are not made of plastic, but they are often held in a plastic casing that can be recycled.

Keys

Your keyboard is recyclable and can go through the shredding practice to be sold as mixed plastic scrap.

Should You Buy a New Energy-Efficient Laptop?

Consider this scenario: Your current laptop is three years old and still operating well, but you notice a new, sleek energy-efficient laptop on the market. Would this new laptop lower your overall carbon emissions? Should you make an upgrade?

A recent study from the Öko-Institut found that manufacturing a laptop is where the greatest amount of emissions are created, at 56 percent. If you use your laptop for five years, 215 kilograms (473.9 pounds) of CO_2 will come from the manufacturing but only 138 kilograms (304.2 pounds) from use. If you purchased a new laptop that was 10 percent more energy efficient than your old one, you would have to use it for 41 years to make up for the production, distribution and disposal emissions. Laptop production also requires a lot of water. It takes an estimated 50,000 liters (13,209 gallons) of water passing through a hydroelectric dam to smelt the aluminum required to make a single laptop.

Swaps and Substitutes: Maintain Your Laptop

A way to minimize plastic waste generated from laptop use is to increase the number of years you use your laptop. One way you can do this is maintenance. Dust buildup can cause your laptop to overheat, potentially damaging your hardware. This also causes your fans to run at full tilt, draining your battery. By regularly cleaning your laptop and removing the internal dust, you can improve your laptop's performance.

If you are in the market for a new device, consider a modular laptop. This way you can replace and upgrade parts instead of doing away with the entire computer.

When getting rid of your old laptop or other electronics, investigate where to dispose of it in your municipality. Many cities have a designated disposal facility for electronic waste, while some businesses, like Best Buy, will collect your old devices.

Dell Computers

Though most laptops end up in the landfill, some companies are leading the way with recycling innovations. Dell Computers is one company that takes in old laptops as inputs for its recycling program. Since 2014 over 125 Dell products have been made with recycled plastic. On top of this, Dell is experimenting with making its packaging completely from recycled plastic, including 25 percent from plastic recovered from the oceans.

Smartphones

The smartphones we use today contain computers more powerful than the ones used to land a man on the moon, and yet we treat these devices as disposable. Americans discard 416,000 cell phones every day. Nearly 152 million are trashed each year. Using data from HYLA Mobile, a mobile device trade-in company, as of 2019 the average age of an iPhone at trade-in was 2.92 years. Today, the average age of a first-time smartphone owner is 10. At this rate the average person living to age 80 will own 24 smartphones over their lifetime.

In 2019 the most popular cell phone model was the iPhone XR, which weighs 194 grams. The specs on what proportion of this phone is made of plastic have not been released, but by using the average that plastics comprise 17 percent of electronics by weight, we can calculate that each phone contains 33 grams (1.2 ounces) of plastic.

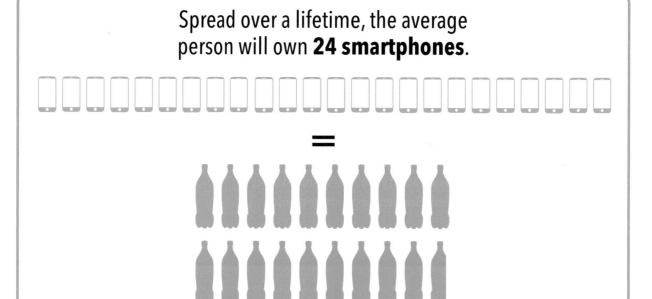

Spread over a lifetime, the average person will own **24 smartphones**.

=

That equals **792 grams (27.9 ounces)** of plastic, which is equivalent to the weight of nearly **20 empty 2-liter bottles**.

Swaps and Substitutes: Secondhand Phones

As the smartphone market continues to expand, so does the secondhand market. As of 2020 used smartphones are valued at around $30 billion. This option diverts e-waste from landfills and can save you money.

When buying secondhand there are some things to consider. If purchasing from an individual, either someone you know or from a listing on a site such as Craigslist, there is the potential to save anywhere between 20 and 90 percent, but you are buying from an unknown seller. Buying from a verified site will cost you more, but the quality of the phone is likely ensured and you might be offered warranties. More companies, including Apple and Samsung, are selling refurbished phones.

Phone Cases

One survey found that 86 percent of smartphone users have a phone case. The bulk of these are made of plastic, and if they aren't then they are then likely packaged in plastic. About 50 percent of phone users also use a screen protector, a thin plastic barrier intended to limit scratches and cracks on the phone's screen.

Should you ditch these plastic phone accessories? Probably not. Though they add to the plastic waste stream, they can protect your phone, which reduces the number of replacement phones you may need to purchase. The phone itself is much more resource intensive.

Why Not Repair?

It would seem that an easy solution to reducing our e-waste is to repair and maintain our devices so that we can extend their life spans. Sadly, repairing is becoming increasingly difficult often because of obstacles put in place by manufacturers, such as Apple. The company, which sold 217 million iPhones in 2018, will not provide you or independent retailers with the tools or instructions to repair its devices. It uses special screws that can only be opened at the Apple Store and even installed a chip in MacBooks that detects third-party repairs and causes the device to lock down. Apple is certainly not the only company to make repairs difficult and also expensive — encouraging consumers to avoid the hassle and buy new.

Another way manufacturers discourage consumers repairing devices is through "planned obsolescence." This is a design strategy to put artificial limits on the useful life of a product so that it becomes either unfashionable or nonfunctional. One way companies do this is by releasing the latest must-have software update that is only compatible with a newer machine.

The Dangers of E-waste Recycling

We are continuing to buy more and more electronics, but only a fraction is recycled. So when you do recycle your old devices, what happens to them? For starters, it's important to note that our old waste is basically a gold mine. Literally! One metric ton of e-waste contains more gold than 7 metric tons of mined gold ore. On top of that, there are a suite of other valuable minerals, such as silver, palladium, platinum, aluminum and copper. As of 2016 there was an estimated value of $55 billion in materials that could be recovered from e-waste — that's more than the GDP of most countries in the world.

In Accra, Ghana, young men burn cables from computers and other electronics in order to recover the copper.

The problem is that extraction is quite laborious, expensive and dangerous work, so removing mineral resources from electronics often takes place in countries with lax labor and environmental laws. Approximately 90 percent of exported e-waste lands in Asia. Workers melt down electronics at a high heat and scrape gold and copper into bins. The process of melting down these and other minerals leads to the emission of dioxin fumes, which can result in long-term health issues, including lesions, brain disorders and cancer. There is pressure for wealthier nations to take responsibility for their own e-waste and extract mineral resources in a more ethical, albeit expensive, way. This issue has long been discussed, and since 1992 an international treaty called the Basel Convention has tried to restrict the flow of e-waste across borders. This has been ratified by more than 180 countries, but not the United States.

Toys

Not only are toys beloved and fun, but also they help us grow and develop. Today, 90 percent of all toys are made of plastic. This is a recent change. The popularity of this material took hold after World War II, when materials like wood, metal and rubber were under rations. This gave toymakers a push to source new materials. Plastic, as a cheap and uncomplicated material, caused a drop in the price of several goods, including toys, and following the postwar baby boom, the demand for toys surged.

Since then, kids have come to own a lot of toys. The toy industry is massive, with over $20 billion in annual sales in the

U.S. alone. One American study investigated the toy habits of children between the ages of 2 and 12 and found that a single child received an average of 71 toys, worth $6,617. A fifth of the households surveyed had more than 100 toys, and one in 10 homes had more than 200. A separate survey conducted in the UK resulted in even greater estimates. It found that children had an average of 238 toys, even though parents estimated that their children played with just 12 favorite toys on a regular basis.

There seems to be an infinite number of toys on the market of all shapes and sizes. For toy manufacturer Hasbro, two-thirds of its portfolio is new each year. This makes it difficult to calculate the average amount of plastic we cycle through when it comes to toys. Instead we will use the weight of the classic toy Mr. Potato Head to represent the average amount of plastic we use just on toys. Made entirely of plastic, Mr. Potato Head and all of his accessories weigh 295 grams (10.4 ounces).

The iconic Mr. Potato Head, made all the more popular by Disney's *Toy Story* franchise, is over 70 years old. First crafted by Hasbro in 1949, the original Mr. Potato Head used an actual potato as the base. It wasn't until 1964, when parents complained of finding moldy potatoes under their children's beds, that Hasbro introduced a large plastic potato body. Since then over 100 million Mr. and Mrs. Potato Heads have been sold in 30 countries.

The average child will own **71 toys** over their lifetime.

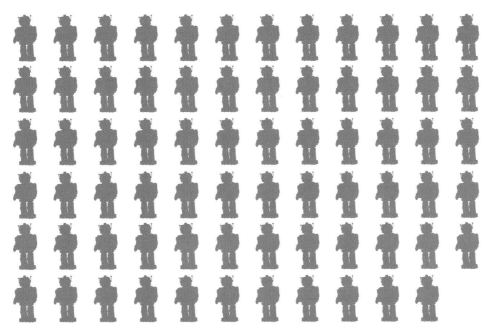

That equals **20.9 kilograms (46.1 pounds)** of plastic.

There is some concern around plastic toys and toxicity. Though highly regulated in some nations, many toys still contain BPA and phthalates, which is a particular concern since children so often put toys in their mouths. (See Chapter 1, page 26 for more on BPA and phthalates.)

The problem with our toys is most of them end up in the landfill. Because they are often a mix of different materials, they are difficult to recycle. The good news is that toys often stay in circulation for a long time: some reports find they last 15 to 20 years before entering the waste stream. One survey of 2,000 parents found that 81 percent repurpose some of their kids' toys. Building blocks, educational toys and bikes were the items most commonly passed down to another child. Nearly six out of 10 parents still have toys that were passed down to them through generations.

Swaps and Substitutes: Experiences and Secondhand Toys

Though toys are important, it's likely that the little one in your life already has more than enough. Next time you are purchasing a gift for a child consider an experience or activity you can share together, such as seeing a movie, going to a museum, attending a sporting event or having a special lunch with just the two of you. Activities can also be free or fairly affordable, such as going for a hike, baking cookies or making playdough from scratch.

When you are looking for new toys, see what you can source from friends and family as they likely have items they are willing

Video Games

Video games are part of the toy world and are also largely made of plastic — from the outer shell, to the controllers, to the cases each game comes in. Sixty-seven percent of Americans, or 211 million people, play video games, and 80 percent of households own a gaming device/ console. In recent years the most popular console release has been the Nintendo Switch, with over 52 million sold by the end of 2019.

Like most toys, video game consoles can stay with us for a long time. There is also high demand for "retro" games on the secondary market. Before scrapping your old gaming systems consider reselling or donating them.

A gamer plays *Fortnite* on his Nintendo Switch.

Less is More

We know that toys are important for child development, but how many toys does a child actually need? A recent study from the University of Toledo invited 36 toddlers (and their parents, of course) to play in a room for 30 minutes. Children were split into two groups. Toddlers in Group 1 were each given 16 toys to play with. Toddlers in Group 2 were only given four. The children provided with just four toys played with each toy for longer and more creatively — in other words, the quality of play was rated higher.

to offload. There are also many avenues to purchase toys secondhand.

If you want to offer toys made from alternative materials, try wooden toys. The first written reference to a wooden toy dates back to 500 BCE (a wooden yo-yo from ancient Greece), and they remain a durable and biodegradable option. If the toys are colorful, be sure to look on the label for food-grade dyes or sealants and paints that are water-based. Conventional paint may include lead, which can lead to serious cognitive impairments.

In addition to wood, many ancient toys were made of clay, like this bird toy, which is on display in the Museum of Cycladic Art in Athens, Greece.

Skipping the Toy with a Meal

A free toy has long been a part of fast-food kids' meals. But these toys are often played with for mere moments before being discarded, and some are never removed from their plastic wrappers before making their way to the garbage. With this in mind, Burger King has promised to stop including non-biodegradable toys in kids meals by 2025. Other fast food chains are beginning to follow suit. In some McDonald's locations kids are offered a choice of a toy or a book.

Textiles

A textile is woven material or cloth. The textile industry is massive and includes clothing, furniture, carpets and linens, such as sheets and towels. Though once dominated by natural fibers, like cotton, today 63 percent of textiles are made from plastic fibers, 26 percent from cotton and the remaining 11 percent is a mix of other materials. As mentioned in Chapter 2, production of synthetic textile fibers uses substantial carbon emissions. With this in mind, the textile industry (natural fibers included) creates 1.2 billion metric tons of CO_2 annually — equivalent to all international flights and maritime shipping combined. On top of this, textile dyeing is the second-largest polluter of water globally after agriculture, contributing 17 to 20 percent of total industrial water pollution.

With each passing year, textile waste is increasing. Every second, one garbage truck of textiles is taken to the landfill or burned. In the U.S., textiles make up 7.6 percent of landfill waste, and in North America the average person disposes of 37 kilograms (81.6 pounds) of textiles annually — that means 9.5 million metric tons accumulate in landfills every year. Fashion is a huge part of the plastic problem and, therefore, takes up the bulk of this section. But first, we examine our use of furniture, carpets and linens.

Furniture

Some furniture can stay in a family for generations, but others have shorter life spans. One study estimates that a couch stays in a home for approximately 11 years. If you buy your first couch when you are 20, you may cycle through an estimated seven couches in your life. But this number might be an underestimate as "fast furniture" has made furniture more affordable and, therefore, more disposable. In 1960 Americans disposed of 1.8 million metric tons of furniture; today that number has jumped to 10.9 million metric tons — an increase that exceeds population growth. Though a portion of furniture waste is incinerated for energy recovery (20 percent), the bulk is landfilled (80 percent).

Wastewater containing dye from a textile factory pours into the Yangtze River. Textile dyeing is one of the major polluters of global waterways.

Swaps and Substitutes: Rethink Your Furniture

The following are ideas to consider when bringing home a new piece of furniture.

- **Buy furniture that's easy to disassemble**. Unlike an office chair made of dozens of layered materials, furniture that can be easily separated into its various raw materials is not only easier to recycle, it is easy to repair.
- **Take care**. When we take good care of our goods they last longer. Investigate the care instructions for your couch and learn how to remove various stains.
- **Buy secondhand**. Purchasing secondhand can help divert a lot of furniture from the landfill. Goods made decades earlier, before the era of fast furniture, are likely to be higher quality.
- **Buy Local**. By purchasing furniture from a local maker, you reduce greenhouse gas emissions. Not only does the final good have less distance to travel, but there is also an increased likelihood that materials were sourced locally.
- **Look at different materials**. Consider buying furniture made from materials other than plastic, but be sure to critically investigate the impact of those materials as well. For example, globally we face deforestation, but this is mainly in tropical areas. A chair made from local hardwoods has significantly less impact than one made from tropical trees. Some species of bamboo (which is actually a grass) can grow an inch every 40 minutes. This fast growth rate makes it easier to maintain bamboo forests. However, bamboo uses a lot of water, and the glue used to piece bamboo products together often contains formaldehyde. Whether this building material is a better swap is up for debate.

Carpet

According to the EPA, every year we throw away 3 million metric tons of carpeting, which is about 1 to 2 percent of landfill waste. Divided across the nation, that is equivalent to every person tossing out roughly 21 pounds of carpet a year. On average, carpets found in homes are made of 92 to 94 percent plastic, but commercial carpets are likely made from 100 percent plastic fibers.

Office Furniture

It may surprise you, but a recent Environmental Protection Agency (EPA) report found that 8 million metric tons of office furniture are discarded as waste each year. It's difficult to calculate the amount of plastic in this waste as many pieces are composites of materials. For example, a cubicle can weigh anywhere between 136 kilograms (300 pounds) and 317 kilograms (700 pounds), and the majority of its materials are a mix of metal, wood and plastic fibers. Meanwhile your office chair might be made of dozens of materials, which makes it nearly impossible to recycle.

Modular carpet tiles are popular in office and commercial settings, but there are many options for homes as well, which can be easily installed.

Swaps and Substitutes: Modular Carpet

The next time you purchase new carpet, consider carpet tiles, also known as "modular carpet." Although this type of carpet initially requires more material, as it requires a thicker backing, it can save a significant amount of material in the long run. Why? Worn or soiled tiles can be swapped out for new tiles without having to replace the entire carpet.

Alternatively, look for manufacturers who make carpet from 100 percent postconsumer content. These rely on end-of-life take-back programs, which are better places to send your rugs than a landfill.

Linens

The EPA data on towels, sheets and pillowcases found that 910,000 metric tons of linens were landfilled in 2015. This makes sense when a survey of 1,000 people found that over half of participants buy new linens every year.

Swaps and Substitutes: Linens

A French study investigated the life span of eight different types of bedsheets. Some of the sheets were made from cotton, some from a polyester blend. Others were made with an "easy-care" treatment that reduces the need for ironing and were dyed either dark or light. The study concluded that no single bedsheet had a significantly better environmental impact. The easy-care treatment meant using more chemicals to create wrinkle-free sheets (which has a negative environmental impact), but the treatment prolonged the wear of the sheets and removed the need for ironing, which saves energy. When comparing light and dark sheets, those dyed light retained color 1.5 times longer than the dark sheets (meaning they didn't appear to need replacing and so were perceived to be of higher quality).

Clothes

In 2015, annual clothing sales had nearly doubled from a decade prior — from $1 trillion to $1.8 trillion — and they are projected to rise to $2.1 trillion by 2025. Compared to two decades ago, we purchase over 400 percent more clothing per year. In 2014, the average North American purchased 16 kilograms (13.2 pounds) of new clothing — that's equivalent to 64 T-shirts or 16 pairs of jeans. If you consider that over 60 percent of clothing today is made from plastic fibers, then we purchase 9.6 kilograms (21.1 pounds) of plastic a year just for our closets.

Spread over a lifetime, the average person will generate **768 kilograms (1,693.2 pounds)** of plastic from clothes.

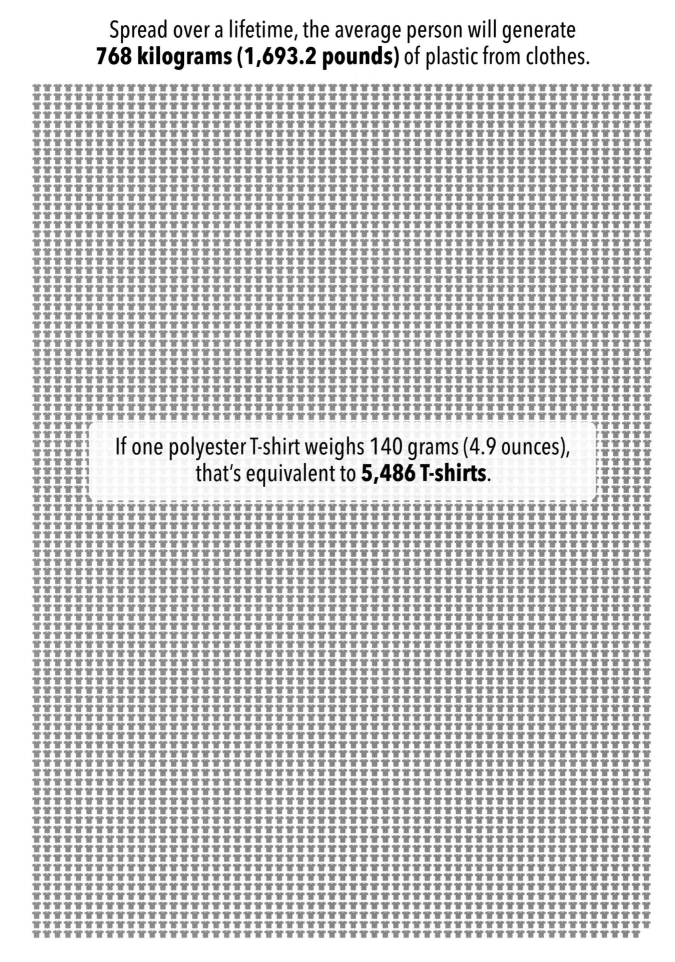

If one polyester T-shirt weighs 140 grams (4.9 ounces), that's equivalent to **5,486 T-shirts**.

The collapse of Rana Plaza, an eight-story garment factory in Dhaka, Bangladesh, exposed the dangers of fashion. Considered the worst accident in the fashion industry's history, Rana Plaza had four floors that were constructed without building permits. When the building collapsed in 2013, it killed 1,134 people and injured over 2,500.

This estimate includes your baby and childhood years; though your clothes were much smaller, your growing body cycled through outfits much more quickly.

Yet this overconsumption is not spread equally across the planet. The global average for purchasing new clothes is 5 kilograms (11 pounds) per year. In the Middle East and Africa, only 2 kilograms (4.4 pounds) is purchased per person every year. In China the average person purchases 6 kilograms (13.2 pounds) worth, and this figure is expected to grow anywhere from 11 kilograms (24.3 pounds) to 16 kilograms (35.3 pounds) by 2030.

As purchasing increases, so does our waste. Worldwide the number of times we wear a garment before we dispose of it has decreased by 36 percent compared to 15 years ago. One survey of 2,000 women in the UK found that garments were worn just seven times before being discarded.

By 2030 it is predicted that the fashion industry will dispose of 134 million metric tons of waste, use 118 billion cubic liters (31.2 trillion gallons) of water and have a carbon footprint of 2.5 billion metric tons of CO_2. These damages can be heavily linked to the rise of fast fashion.

Fast Fashion

Since 2000 there has been an immense expansion of fast fashion, which is defined as "inexpensive clothing made rapidly by mass-market retailers in response to the latest trends." Some of the brands leading this expansion include Zara, H&M and Fashion Nova. Though cheap, these articles come at a high price: the quality is often poor (causing the clothing to wear out rapidly), the clothing's impact on the environment is severe and the health and safety of workers are far-too-often jeopardized. The average garment worker in Bangladesh, the second-biggest garment-producing nation after China, makes just $64 a month in wages.

Fast fashion would not be possible without polyester. Over 21 million metric tons of this cheap plastic fabric were used in 2016 — that's a 157 percent increase since 2000. In 2015 this fiber generated 282 million metric tons of CO_2 emissions just to produce it. Not only that but also this fabric does not break down in the same way as natural fibers and will remain on our planet as waste for as many as 200 years.

High Fashion: Not So Innocent

Though fast fashion may be the leading culprit for our increased fashion waste, high fashion isn't blameless. In July 2018 luxury fashion brand Burberry admitted to burning almost $40 million of its unsold clothes, accessories and perfume instead of selling them to wholesale markets. Though it's one of the first brands to address this publicly, it has long been suspected that high-end brands destroy their unsold stock to protect the brand's exclusivity and value.

What Happens When You Donate Your Clothes?

Estimates suggest that 95 percent of clothing could be used again — either reworn, repurposed or recycled — but sadly the majority ends up thrown in the garbage. Only about 13 percent of clothes are donated, but what really happens when you donate your used clothes?

For starters 30 to 40 percent of donated clothes end up in local or regional secondhand stores. The remainder is shipped overseas and sold internationally. In 2014, 4.3 million metric tons of used clothes were traded internationally, primarily to developing nations. That number is beginning to fall. With the emergence of fast fashion, importers are less willing to accept hand-me-downs because the quality of clothing has lowered. A portion of clothes that cannot be resold internationally can be "downcycled" into cleaning rags or insulation, but a large percentage is burned, as countries importing clothes often do not have the waste management facilities to deal with textiles. If the quality of clothing continues to fall, demand will continue to decrease.

Workers in Senegal load bundles of secondhand clothing from Europe and America onto the roof of a bus.

Downcycling vs. Upcycling

Within the waste sector you will sometimes hear the terms "downcycle" and "upcycle." Downcycling refers to the practice of turning materials into new products but usually those of lower value, such as turning a sweater into rags. Upcycling is when discarded materials are turned into products of higher quality and value. An example is taking a discarded table, and sanding and staining it to make it look new.

In terms of recycling, only 3 percent of all garments are turned into something else: 2 percent are downcycled into rags and insulation, and only 1 percent is truly recycled — meaning old clothing fibers are broken down and turned into new fibers for new clothes. Experts estimate that by not recycling old clothing in this way, we are losing more than $100 billion worth of material each year. One reason so little is recycled is the complexity of garments. Buttons, zippers and other non-textile parts need to be removed. Colors, coatings and prints also create several challenges, but the biggest obstacle is blended fabrics. For example, your favorite sweater might be made of 50 percent cotton and 50 percent polyester. Before this sweater can be recycled, the fabrics need to be separated. While this process is technically possible (for example, cotton will not dissolve under alkaline conditions, but polyester will), it is still in the trial stage. As things currently stand it is often cheaper for a manufacturer to make garments from new materials than recycled ones.

So what should you do? Are you donating your clothes in vain? Experts say to keep donating. Even gently used socks and underwear that are not ripped or stained can be donated to local

From Laundry to Sea

Of course, most plastic pollution comes from the things we throw away, but did you know 500,000 metric tons of plastic are entering the ocean through a surprising source? The answer is your laundry machine. As you know over 60 percent of textiles are made of plastic fibers. When we wash our clothes and linens, tiny fibers fall off. Think of the lint tray in your dryer — the same thing is happening in your washer. One study found that acrylic fibers fall off with the greatest frequency and can release over 700,000 fibers in a single load of laundry. Microfibers are considered a form of microplastics, and one study estimated that microfibers make up 35 percent of the microplastic in the ocean. These fibers can end up negatively impacting aquatic animals by blocking digestion and acting as rafts for different bacteria.

If you're interested in reducing the number of

A front-loading washing machine is a better option for keeping plastic fibers out of wastewater.

fibers you release into our waterways but still want your clothes to be clean, there are things you can do. First, aim to use a front-loading washer. Top-loading washers release seven times more fibers, and front-loading washers use less water and the tumbling is less intense. Most wastewater treatment centers do not use filters fine enough to remove these fibers, but there are now filters on the market that you can add to your machine.

Shoes

According to the American Apparel and Footwear Association, Americans (including children) buy 7.5 pairs of shoes a year. Stretched over a lifetime that is roughly 600 pairs. In terms of materials, leather, textiles (typically cotton and polyester), rubber (either natural or made from polyester) and foam (made primarily from polyurethane plastic) are the most popular. Clearly, plastic plays a big role in the shoe industry. Shoes are incredibly diverse and made of many materials and components. At its simplest, a flip-flop is made of two parts while some sneakers could be made from over 60 parts. Like so many items made with plastic, this complex mixing of materials makes recycling difficult, so 95 percent of shoes are landfilled at the end of their life.

charities and shelters. For clothing items that have seen better days you can contact your local recycling center and inquire about textile recycling in your area.

We know we cannot continue sending bales of unwanted clothing overseas, and experts suggest we should see this time as an opportunity to innovate. By consulting with different manufacturing sectors, such as the automotive, carpeting, paper and building sectors, there is potential for better end markets for our discarded textiles.

Swaps and Substitutes: Sustainable Fashion

Could the antidote to fast fashion lie in sustainable fashion? First thing's first, many even debate the term "sustainable fashion" since much of fashion is all about following ever-changing trends, which itself encourages near continual consumption. Despite these semantics, there are real options to create a more sustainable wardrobe.

Dr. Anna Brismar, an expert in circular fashion, has identified six pillars of sustainable fashion, all of which can and should be combined:

- **Shop green and clean**. Gravitate toward clothing that is produced in an environmentally conscious way at every stage of its life cycle. This approach considers what resources are used, how those resources impact water and habitat, how textiles are prepared and dyed, how the clothing is distributed and disposed of, and the carbon emissions associated with each of these factors.
- **Look for high quality and timeless design**. Though fashion is always changing, some pieces remain classics. Classics can be specific to you — what makes you look and feel good.

Purchasing well-made items that you truly love means they might stay in your wardrobe your entire life. Unsure if you love a shirt? Put it back. Take a week and think about if you really want it. Often we can reduce our waste simply by taking some time to decide if we actually like the thing we are about to buy.

- **Shop fair, ethical and local.** It is only possible for fast fashion to be so cheap because somewhere along the line people are being treated unethically. Behind every $10 sweater is often unfair wages or dangerous working conditions. Consider the ethical practices of a brand before making a purchase. Also consider *where* you purchase your clothes. Try and skip online shopping to avoid the added CO_2 emissions, and whenever possible consider shopping from a small business to support your local economy.
- **Repair, redesign and upcycle.** Like all goods, taking care of them through cleaning and repair means they will stay in your closet longer. If an item no longer appeals to you in the same way, consider upcycling or redesigning it in a way that fits your style.
- **Rent, borrow and swap.** The shared economy is growing, and there are now more options to rent clothes. Businesses such as Rent the Runway and Gwynnie Bee allow you to indulge in the latest trends without the commitment. Some sustainability experts argue that the environmental footprint from dry cleaning and deliveries negate the positives, while others see it as step in the right direction. Alternatively, you can share on a more local scale, like organizing a clothing swap with friends.
- **Buy secondhand and vintage.** Purchasing secondhand keeps clothing out of landfills and decreases the environmental impact associated with making new clothes. Can't seem to give up online shopping? There are now retailers, such as thredUP, that operate online thrift stores.

Sashiko, a Japanese embroidery technique, has gained popularity as a way to mend clothing and also make something unique to your style.

Sunglasses

When asking how many sunglasses a person owns in their lifetime, a better question might be how many does a person lose? It's one of the most frequently lost items we carry with us. In fact, Disney World has kept a record of lost items since 1971 and estimates over 1.65 million pairs have found their way to the lost and found. On average, 210 pairs are turned in daily.

Since the frequency at which you lose your sunnies is so variable, we'll use a recommendation from scientists. The results of one study out of Brazil suggests that sunglasses should be replaced every two years — any longer and the UV protection begins to degrade. They tested this by placing different pairs in front of a sun simulator lamp. Though glasses can be made from a mix of materials, including metal and glass, most have lenses and frames made from plastic.

Think you own a lot of eyewear? Elton John revealed in a BBC interview that he owns 250,000 pairs of glasses (sunglasses included).

Starting from childhood, the average person will use **40 pairs of sunglasses** in a lifetime.

If one pair weighs 30 grams (1 ounce), that equals **1.2 kilograms (2.6 pounds)** of plastic.

Swaps and Substitutes: Sunglass Strap

Though whether it is a fashionable option is up for debate, a sunglass strap is a simple addition you can add to your favorite pair of sunglasses. A strap can help reduce the number of sunglasses you lose, minimizing the need to purchase replacement pairs.

Calculating Your Lifetime-Use Plastic Footprint

More than exact numbers and specific metrics, calculating your plastic footprint is about understanding your habits as a consumer and reevaluating your relationship with the things you buy and use. It can be difficult to determine exactly how much plastic is in, say, your car or your desk chair, and in a way trying to figure that out distances you from the point. What is far more important is for you to reflect on *how many* cars and desk chairs you run through over your lifetime, *why* you run through that many and how you can rethink your relationship with those items.

One way you can go about understanding your plastic footprint is by doing an audit of the long-term plastic items you use.

Lifetime-Use Plastic Audit

A plastic audit may sound fairly simply, but there are a number of factors to consider. You might use this chapter as a starting point, but if you think about the objects in your home or at your job that are completely or at least partially made of plastic, you'll know that the list of items we've included is merely scratching the surface. Given the scale of how much plastic exists in our day-to-day lives, we couldn't even touch on things such as appliances, construction materials, kitchenware and numerous other objects that you interact with on a daily basis. Rather than cataloging every plastic item in your home (which could be an impossible task), perhaps narrow your audit to the long-term items you replace most frequently.

Furthermore, the data we presented is based on averages, and it's likely those averages don't exactly reflect your own use. It's important, then, to record how many of a specific item you own or have owned, and from that number you can roughly calculate how frequently you replace something.

For example, if you're 40 years old and you've owned four cars in the past 22 years (since you turned 18), you can divide 22 by 4 to find out that, on average, you've replaced your car every 5.5 years. If you plan to drive for another 40 years and replace your car at the same rate, in your lifetime you will have owned nearly 11 cars. To get this number, simply divide the total number of years you expect to use a specific type of item (in this case, from when you're 18 until you're 80, so 62 years) by your rate of replacement. Using some of the categories we covered in this chapter, your audit might look a bit like this:

Item	Rate of replacement	Expected total number of years of use	Number of items you will use over your lifetime
Car	Every 5.5 years	62 years	10.9
Laptop	Every 6.5 years	62 years	9.5
Smartphone	Every 2.5 years	60 years	24
Couch	Every 7 years	55 years	7.8
Sunglasses	Every 2 years	70 years	35

Though your needs and habits will likely change as you get older, this list is designed to give you a rough sense of how many plastic-containing items you will use in your life. Take some time to reflect on what that pile of items looks like and means to you.

- How much space in the global trash pile will these items take up?
- Are you OK with the number of each type of item you will buy in your lifetime?
- How can you reduce the number of items or the impact they have on the environment? Recall some of the 6 Rs (see Chapter 3, pages 48–52).

The purpose of this exercise is not to make you feel guilty about how many plastic-containing items you have used in your life; it is a tool to help you understand where most of your plastic consumption is coming from and to think critically about your habits. From here you can choose to change your habits and make effective, lifelong strides to reduce your plastic footprint.

CHAPTER 5

Single-Use and Short-Term-Use Plastic

P lastic is an incredibly durable material, strong enough to last multiple lifetimes, and yet approximately half of all the plastic we make is used only once and then thrown away. Referred to as "single-use plastic," this type of waste is at the forefront of the plastic problem. Since we often throw single-use items away with little thought, it might feel like an insignificant amount, but what if we each stacked up this waste over the course of our lifetime?

This chapter explores common single-use items that might be a part of your plastic footprint, and it also assesses alternatives and the merits of these swaps and substitutes. Our individual efforts to reduce our plastic waste are important, but it's also essential that we investigate alternatives with a critical lens. The different materials that comprise these swaps each have their pros and cons. For example, you can purchase a reusable straw made of stainless steel, glass, bamboo and several other materials, but these have their own environmental footprint. Here, the positives and negatives are evaluated where research is available.

Swaps and Substitutes Guidelines

No matter what the substitute, consider the following guidelines before switching to a new item:

- **Go with reusable**. Whenever possible, go with a swap you can use again and again. Swapping a single-use plastic bag for a brown paper bag might be a good option (the paper bag is easily recycled and will biodegrade), but it has its own set of environmental impacts (such as use of water resources, deforestation and habitat degradation). In this instance, a reusable cloth bag that you use for many years and repair is the better option.
- **Refill**. If available and accessible in your community, visit bulk stores where you can bring your own containers.
- **Buy big**. Sometimes bigger is better. If you have favorite items but they are packaged in plastic, you can minimize waste by buying the "family sized" option. Because of the surface area-to-volume ratio, four small containers will be the same volume

A number of bulk food stores will allow you to bring your own containers and/or reusable bags.

as one large container but double the surface area (i.e., more plastic packaging). However, you should only buy big if this is a product you know you like and will use up. Otherwise you might end up creating more waste by buying things you don't need or want.

■ **Use it up**. Before you make a swap to a new eco-minded product, make sure the items you already own aren't going to waste. For example, use up your remaining liquid shampoo before transitioning to your zero-waste shampoo bar.

Straws

The straw has become the face of single-use plastic waste. A big reason for this is a viral 2015 video of a sea turtle with a plastic straw lodged in its nose. The video documented the straw's painful removal by a marine biologist. The clip has been viewed over 40 million times and has sparked a lot of anger. Since this video was posted, plastic waste has become a central environmental concern.

Straws, weighing less than half a gram, represent only 0.0025 percent of the total marine litter volume. But in the past 30 years of the International Coastal Cleanup, volunteers have picked up over 9 million straws off beaches. An estimated 500 million straws are used in American restaurants, hotels and homes daily. They are a part of our daily lives, with every person using an estimated 1.6 straws per day.

This powerful viral video of a turtle having a staw pulled out of its nose brought our planet's plastic problem to the fore.

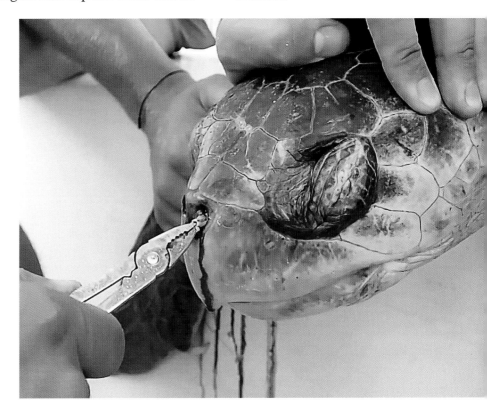

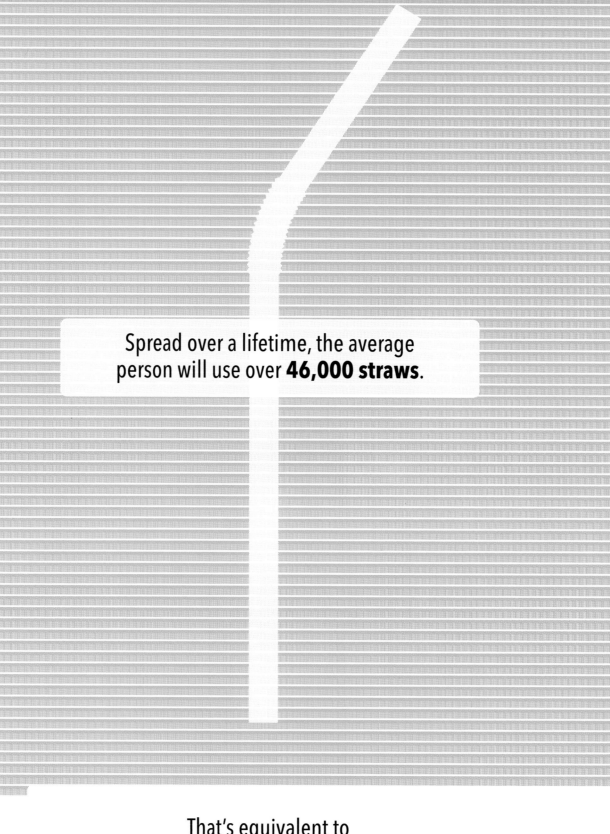

Spread over a lifetime, the average person will use over **46,000 straws**.

That's equivalent to
22 kilograms (48.5 pounds) of plastic waste.

#StopSucking

Plastic straw bans are gaining momentum in several cities and countries. Several companies, such as Starbucks and Disney theme parks, have committed to phasing out straws from stores. Talk of bans gained a lot of traction on social media with the hashtag #StopSucking being used by celebrities like Neil deGrasse Tyson, Tom Brady and Sonam Kapoor.

Swaps and Substitutes: Reusable Straws

Reusable straws seem to be the simple swap for single-use plastic straws, as they limit the amount of litter that enters the environment, but there are several different kinds on the market and other environmental factors, such as energy expenditure and emissions, to consider. How do reusable straws stack up?

A study from Humboldt State University compared stainless steel, glass and bamboo straws then measured how many times you would need to use them to make up both energy expenditure and CO_2 emissions.

	Plastic straw	Stainless steel straw	Glass straw	Bamboo straw
Embedded energy (kJ/straw)	23.7	2,420	1,074	756
CO_2 emissions (grams of CO_2/straw)	1.46	217	65.2	38.8
Straw reuses needed to pay off embedded energy	Disposable	102	45	32
Straw reuses needed to pay off CO_2	Disposable	149	45	27

From this analysis it might appear like you should skip the stainless steel straw, but it's less likely to break than a glass or bamboo version, so you might get more miles. The main takeaway is whatever reusable straw you choose, be sure to actually use it as it takes significant resources and energy to make.

The Problem with Pens

Like straws, plastic pens present similar risks to marine life. While not much information is available about how big the disposable plastic pen problem is, some sources estimate that Americans throw away as many as 1.6 billion pens each year.

A father helps his son drink from a cup using a plastic straw. For many, plastic straws are the best option because of their flexibility.

Perhaps the best option is to skip the straw altogether. Remember you can refuse a straw with your drink if you don't need or want it.

A Necessity for Many

With straw bans emerging throughout the world, disability scholars and advocates remind us that plastic straws are a necessity for many. The flexible bend in a plastic straw was designed to aid people in hospitals with drinking, and this universal design has helped many with different abilities. Some who are unable to lift a cup to their mouth require a straw to drink, and reusable straws do not work as an alternative for many. Paper or pasta straws can be choking hazards, and metal, bamboo or glass straws can pose higher risks of injuries and cannot be repositioned. When evaluating how to manage plastic waste, it's important to consider how such changes impact everyone, not just the majority.

Plastic Bags

Plastic bags were invented in the 1950s, and by the 1980s they were increasingly replacing paper bags. Scientists estimate that we use 1 to 5 trillion plastic bags every year globally. If we take the higher estimate, that is 10 million bags per minute. The surface area of 5 trillion bags could cover France twice over. Different nations use plastic bags at different rates. In Denmark, shoppers use approximately four bags every year. Meanwhile in the U.S., the average shopper uses about one a day. Here are more bags-per-person averages for other countries around the world:

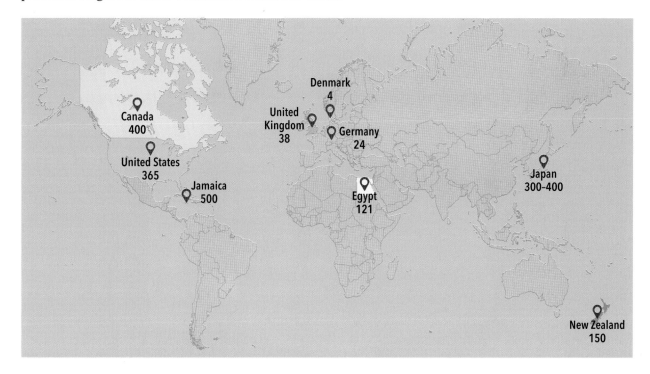

Though variable in size and shape, on average a bag weighs 5 grams. These bags, mostly made from polyethylene, are great for carrying items because they are lightweight, durable and strong. But they are also incredibly damaging to the environment for those same reasons. The lightweight and balloon-like design means they can be blown into the land and sea easily. Their durability means they will be on our planet for a long time — some scientists estimate 1,000 years. And though they don't break down, they can break apart into microplastics.

Plastic bag bans as well as fees have been implemented in several cities and countries. The effectiveness of this strategy is discussed in Chapter 3 on pages 63–65.

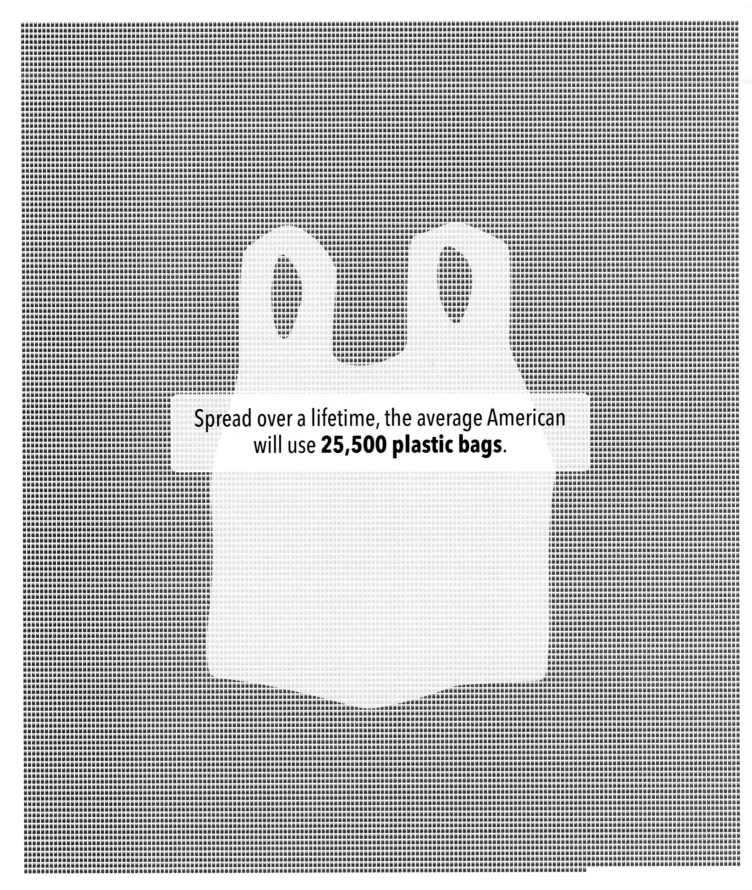

Spread over a lifetime, the average American will use **25,500 plastic bags**.

That's equivalent to
128 kilograms (282.2 pounds) of plastic waste.

Swaps and Substitutes: Reusable Bags

A reusable tote or bag seems like a winning swap. However, a life cycle assessment written by the Danish Environmental Protection Agency challenges this assumption. The report found that cotton totes were more detrimental to climate change, water use and air pollution than their single-use plastic counterparts. They found that a cotton bag would need to be reused 1,000 times to be as sustainable as using single-use bags. The problem is this analysis did not include the impact plastic has on the natural environment once it's thrown away. As discussed, that impact is huge, with an estimated 100,000 marine mammals dying annually from plastic debris.

So what should you do? When we investigate how many single-use bags we use in a lifetime (25,500), it's equivalent to over 25 cotton totes in terms of their environmental impact from production. Chances are you do not need that many bags. So as long as you aren't buying every cute tote you see and you make sure you use it over and over for many years, you should feel confident in your reusable bag swap. Another way you can curb your impact is to refer to the 6 Rs in Chapter 3 or the swap guidelines at the beginning of this chapter. Could you buy one secondhand? Does a friend have one that they are no longer using? Can you make one out of an old shirt you no longer wear? Get creative!

There will be times when you forget your bag and need a plastic one. Just be sure to reuse that bag. Bring it to the supermarket with you next time, use it to line your garbage pail or pack your lunch in it. Turn a single-use bag into a multiuse bag.

Disaster, Disease and Death

Though light in weight and small in size, plastic bags can create big problems. They can block waterways during a natural disaster, exacerbating the impact. In Bangladesh, plastic bag litter worsened a flood in 1998 because the bags blocked drainage. Two-thirds of the country was covered in water, and 2,379 people died. This devastating event, made worse by plastic waste, led to banning polyethylene bags in 2002.

In parts of the world with limited waste management facilities, plastic bag litter can help spread disease. Wet plastic bags provide habitats for breeding mosquitoes, which can increase the risk of diseases like malaria.

Residents in Dhaka, Bangladesh, wade through floodwaters in 1998.

Plastic Drinking Bottles

Nearly a million plastic drinking bottles are sold every minute. In 2016 more than 480 billion were purchased worldwide, and this number is expected to jump 20 percent by 2021. Though the plastic used to make most bottles is highly recyclable (polyethylene terephthalate, or PET), fewer than half are collected for recycling, with the majority ending up in landfills or the ocean. In 2015 Americans purchased 11 billion beverages in plastic bottles — that's 346 per person per year. There are a lot of different shapes and sizes, but a 500-milliliter (16.9-ounce) bottle of Coca Cola (the top soft drink brand in the world) made of PET plastic weighs 24 grams (0.8 ounces).

If a person drank 346 beverages in plastic bottles a year, in a lifetime they would use **27,680 bottles**.

That's equivalent to approximately **664 kilograms (1,463.9 pounds)** of plastic waste.

Bottled Water

In 2017 bottled water was the top-selling beverage in America with over 51.8 billion liters (13.7 billion gallons) consumed. Market research experts predict that the market will continue to grow from $199 billion in 2017 to $307 billion by 2024. But for most Americans and many others around the world, water is free. So how did it become a billion-dollar industry?

Experts have broken down a few reasons. Like so many consumer goods, it can be seen as fashionable; consider endorsements of particular bottled water brands by celebrities like Jennifer Aniston, Idris Elba and Mark Wahlberg. Another reason is public access has become increasingly limited; broken or dirty water fountains are continuously more commonplace, which discourages people from using them. Finally, many believe bottled to be safer than tap water, but in most parts of the world the two are equal. In fact, tap water is often more rigorously tested. In the city of Toronto, Ontario, tap water is tested every six hours to make sure harmful bacteria is absent, but there is no government body testing bottled water.

Swaps and Substitutes: Reusable Drinking Bottles

There are many options for reusable drinking bottles, but essentially you can categorize them into three types: stainless steel, glass and plastic. Each has its pros and cons.

Stainless Steel

✓ strong and long lasting
✓ 100 percent recyclable (check your municipality guidelines)
X energy intensive production
X metallic taste

Glass

✓ highly recyclable (unless made with shatterproof glass)
✓ best taste
X breakable
X most expensive

Plastic

✓ strong
✓ least energy to make
X will leach chemicals when exposed to sun/heat
X will not decompose

A Necessity for Many

Though billions of people around the world can turn on their taps to get free, clean water, 780 million do not have access to an "improved water source." According to the World Health Organization, an improved water source isn't just tap water but also includes public standpipes, boreholes, protected dug wells, protected springs and rainwater collection. However, these measures don't always provide safe drinking water, so the number of people without clean water could be substantially higher than 780 million.

Though certainly not a long-term solution, bottled water provides a necessary stop gap for millions around the world.

Coffee and Tea

Billions of people around the world begin their mornings with a hot caffeinated beverage, like coffee or tea. Coffee and tea have been favorite drinks for centuries, with some geographic regions having a preference for one over the other. Plastic is not required to make either of these delicious drinks and yet, because of convenience, plastic waste has become entwined with both.

Coffee

The average American coffee drinker has two cups per day. Over a year that amounts to 730 cups of coffee. Though there are many ways to drink your java, two methods in particular create a lot of waste: coffee pods and takeout coffee cups.

Coffee Pods

There are several brands of coffee pods, but the one you might be most familiar with are the single-serve K-Cups used in Keurig coffee makers. Keurig machines have been around for over 20 years and were originally made for office use. At the time of making the first K-Cup, the inventor, John Sylan, felt the environmental impact would be neutral as it would substitute a takeout coffee cup. What he didn't anticipate was their popularity in homes. Today he regrets his invention and personally doesn't use coffee pods.

Coffee pods are convenient but ultimately create a mound of waste that more likely than not will end up in a landfill or incinerated.

Currently, 40 percent of American households own a single-cup coffee brewing system. Every minute, an estimated 39,000 pods are made, while 29,000 are tossed in landfills. Some estimates state that in a single year the number of discarded pods could wrap around the globe 12 times. Though more companies are migrating to creating pods out of recyclable material, most pods are still unrecyclable or require you to drop them off at the distributor to be recycled at a special facility.

The packaging of a single pod weighs roughly 4 grams (0.14 ounces). If you drank each of your two daily cups of joe using pods, in a year you would produce approximately 3 kilograms (6.6 pounds) of plastic waste.

According to the *New York Times*, K-Cup coffee costs approximately $50 per 454 grams (1 pound). If you drank just one cup a day, you would get through about 3.6 kilograms (8 pounds) of coffee a year. Sure, your Keurig can make a cup in under 30 seconds, but is it worth the yearly price tag of $400?

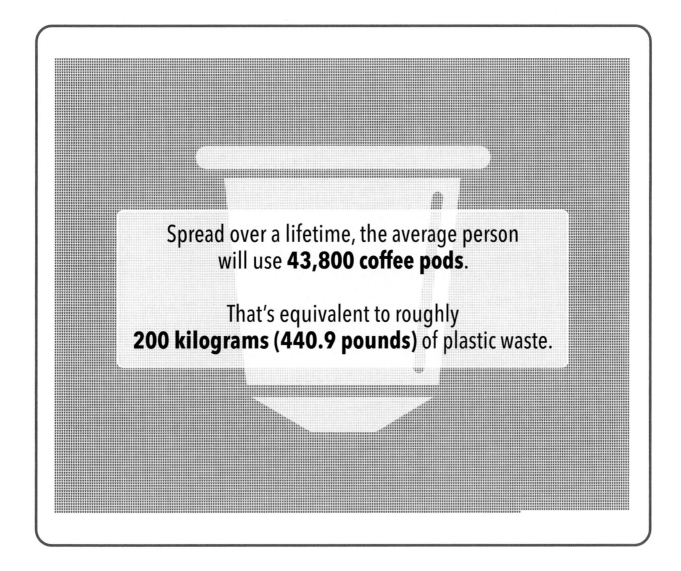

Spread over a lifetime, the average person will use **43,800 coffee pods**.

That's equivalent to roughly **200 kilograms (440.9 pounds)** of plastic waste.

Coffee Cups

Not every coffee we drink is made at home or in the office. A lot of us grab it on the go. Maybe you bring your own cup to your favorite café, but currently less than 5 percent of people use a reusable mug. You might look at a disposable coffee cup and not find it too shameful compared to, say, a plastic water bottle. After all, the cup is made of paper. But within almost every paper cup is a plastic liner that is used to make the cup waterproof and maintain the temperature of the drink. Technically, these cups can be recycled. Facilities exist that are capable of separating the plastic liner from the paper cup, but they are rare and costly. Standard recycling facilities do not have this capability, and this means less than 1 percent of cups are recycled. The rest are landfilled or find their way into the environment.

Every person has different coffee drinking habits, but let's use the number of coffee cups used in the United Kingdom as a basis. In 2011, 2.5 billion cups were thrown away in the UK, a number that researchers estimate has since increased. The UK population in 2011 was 63.18 million, so if those coffees were split evenly across the country, each person would grab a coffee to go 39.5 times a year.

The lining weighs approximately 0.1 grams (0.004 ounces), and the plastic lid weighs an average of 3 grams (0.1 ounces).

Spread over a lifetime, the average person will get **2,567.5 coffee cups** for the road.

That's equivalent to roughly **8 kilograms (17.6 pounds)** of plastic waste.

The paper used to make the cup also has an impact. One study found that each cup emits 0.11 kilograms (0.24 pounds) of CO_2 when production and shipping are considered. Paper cup production also leads to the loss of trees, degrades ecosystems and decreases abilities of forests to absorb carbon.

Swaps and Substitutes:
Try a French Press or Take a Reusable Mug

If you're brewing at home, a pod might be convenient, but it's a pricey and unsustainable option. So what is the most eco-friendly option for brewing a warm cup? Experts recommend a French press (specifically with water boiled by an electric kettle). It requires the least amount of energy and produces minimal waste.

If you're on the go (or you just prefer someone else making your coffee for you), remember to bring a reusable mug. The pros and cons are quite similar to that of a reusable water bottle, but an undeniable pro of any mug is the mutual cost benefit to the buyer and vendor. Usually there is a discount when you bring your own mug, and the vendor spends less money on single-use cups. Below is a cost analysis conducted by the Environmental Protection Agency (EPA):

Assumptions:
- $0.15 — Cost of disposable packaging (cup, lid and sleeve)
- $0.10 — Discount for bringing your own cup
- 12 hours — Daily operating hours

Want Not, Waste Not

When it comes to coffee, making only what you intend on drinking is the best option. Brewing an entire pot of drip coffee but only drinking one cup is much more wasteful than a coffee made with a K-Cup, because the most resources and energy in the entire coffee-producing process go into growing the beans. In fact, the amount of water required to grow, process and transport the beans for a single cup is 140 liters (36.9 gallons) — something to consider when you throw a pot down the drain.

Number of "bring-your-own" cups per hour	Daily cost savings	Annual cost savings	Annual greenhouse gas reductions (in CO_2)*	Annual solid waste reduction*
3	$1.80	$657	149.7 kg (339 lbs)	171.5 kg (378 lbs)
10	$6.00	$2,190	512.6 kg (1,130 lbs)	571.5 kg (1,260 lbs)

* based on a 473.2 milliliter (16 fluid ounce) cup with an insulating sleeve

Tea

The world's most popular beverage, second only to water, is tea. The Food and Agriculture Organization of the United Nations estimates the world drinks six billion cups a day. The Brits, who notoriously love their tea, drink 2.5 cups a day.

For centuries this drink has been prepared with loose leaf tea, and many people still enjoy it this way. However, since its invention in the early 20th century, the tea bag has been dominating the scene.

Tea bags

Historically, tea bags have been made of paper products, silk or cotton. Today many are still made with paper but are sealed with a plastic glue, while others are made entirely of plastic. Most empty tea bags weigh less than 0.5 grams (0.018 ounces). If you start drinking 2.5 cups of tea a day when you're 15, you'll down 59,312.5 cups in your lifetime, and if those bags are made of plastic, that's 30 kilograms (66 pounds) of waste that isn't biodegradable.

What might be more alarming is not how much plastic we throw away but how much we ingest. A 2019 study revealed that steeping a single plastic tea bag at temperatures of 95°C releases approximately 11.6 billion microplastics and 3.1 billion nanoplastics in a

Plastic tea bags, sometimes referred to as silky tea bags, are a hidden source of microplastics in our tea.

single cup. Even though the bags are made of food-grade plastic, they begin to deteriorate in hot water after five minutes.

Ingesting billions of plastic particles sounds serious, but is it any reason for concern? In the same study, scientists exposed water fleas (animals commonly used in toxicity experiments) to the micro and nanoplastics released from tea bags. The plastics were not lethal but impacted their swimming ability and caused their carapace (shell) to swell. Other studies have documented the effects microplastics have had on algae, zooplankton, fish and mice. Some observed that there was potential for cellular uptake once the microplastics were inside the digestive tract — meaning plastic might not just move through our digestive system, it might become part of our cells. However, this is all still speculative and has not been shown in humans. The World Health Organization states that currently there is no evidence of health risks for people.

But when it comes to less waste, there is a clear winner. Loose leaf tea is a simple plastic-free swap.

Strictly speaking, microplastics are plastic particles that range from 100 nanometers (nm) to 5 millimeters (mm), while nanoplastics are anything smaller than 100 nm. Though some plastics are designed to be micro or nano sized, in general these are the outcome of larger plastics breaking apart. Micro and nanoplastics pose numerous challenges: they are difficult to quantify and clean up, and researchers have trouble evaluating their effects on animals and people.

Loose leaf tea with a reusable strainer will produce the least waste. Loose leaf tea can also be purchased in bulk.

Microplastics in Food and Drink

Tea isn't the only time you might sip or munch on plastic. Microplastics have been detected in table salt, with up to 681 particles per kilogram (2.2 pounds). One study found that a third of all fish sampled had ingested plastic, and mussels contain an average of 0.4 microplastics per gram (0.03 ounces). Plastic fibers have been found in our tap water and in 240 different types of water bottles sold commercially around the world. A recent study found that, depending on age and gender, we eat on average one credit card's worth of plastic each week.

Product Packaging

By industry, most plastic is made for the purpose of packaging. Each year, 146 million metric tons are produced — 35.9 percent of all plastic — with the majority of this being used one time and then disposed of. There are many types of product packaging, but below are some particularly tricky types.

Clamshells and Other Blister Packaging

Invented in 1978, clamshells, a type of blister packaging, are made of a single piece of plastic with a hinged design (making it look like a clamshell). Clamshell packaging is popular among retailers because the product is made visible on both sides. One of the downsides is, it can be extremely frustrating to open and has even coined the phrase "wrap rage." Every year thousands of people seek medical treatment from injuries sustained while trying to open this type of plastic packaging. Heat-sealed packaging is particularly difficult to open, as many of these are made to be tamper proof.

Clamshells are not just annoying to open, but also they are difficult to recycle. Though they are frequently made with PET, a highly recyclable plastic, the packages are often covered in strong adhesive stickers that can't be removed, making them ineligible for recycling. They can also be made of PVC, which is not easily recycled.

Blister packaging is in the same "difficult to recycle" category. Think of a pack of batteries with a cardboard backing or a pack of pills with an aluminum foil backing. Separating these materials from the plastic is also hard. These issues, combined with a changing global recycling market (see Chapter 3, page 56), means most of these containers are destined for the landfill. For example, the city of Calgary, Alberta, had been storing 2,000 metric tons of plastic clamshell containers since 2017. The city hoped international recycling markets would stabilize; unfortunately the cost of storing the containers was too costly, at $250,800 ($300,000 Canadian dollars) since 2017, and they have since been sent to the landfill.

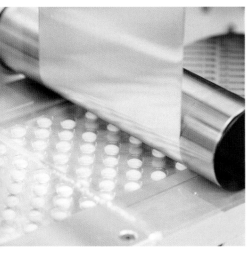

A machine applies a foil backing to blister packaging. The fusing of foil and plastic make this type of packaging very difficult to recycle.

Online Shopping

Since its beginning, online shopping has grown into a multitrillion-dollar industry worldwide. In 2017, 165 billion packages were shipped throughout the U.S., and according to a 2015 survey, eight in 10 Americans have purchased something online, with 15 percent buying online on a weekly basis. This trend comes with a lot more packaging than conventional retail stores, but why?

Traditional retail follows a fairly simple stream: goods are shipped in bulk to a warehouse and then to a store. But with online shopping there are, on average, four times the number of touch points, and shipments are delivered as individual packages. Online shipping also requires a lot of extra cushioning to ensure the safe arrival of your packages. According to one study, the average box is dropped 17 times before arriving on the purchaser's doorstep. Goods are often packed in much larger boxes so that the box can be filled with plastic bags of air, which are designed to keep your purchase protected.

Swaps and Substitutes: Brick-and-Mortar Stores

Ordering items online can be very convenient since you can shop within the comfort of your home (and pajamas). But according to an MIT study, online purchases come with five times the packaging compared to in-store purchases (5.5 times for rush deliveries). Choosing a brick-and-mortar store will

Boxes from online purchases are often filled with extra packaging to cushion purchased goods.

reduce a lot of waste. However, people tend to buy more in a physical store. One report found that 71 percent of shoppers spent more than $50 when in a brick-and-mortar store, but only 54 percent of shoppers did the same online. Stores have clever tactics that encourage impulse buys, and more impulse shopping equals more waste. To help curb impulse buys, create a list before you go on your shopping trip and stick to it. Or consider doing your "window shopping" online first but then making your purchase in a brick-and-mortar store to eliminate waste.

If you must buy online, try to avoid returning items. Online shoppers tend to over-order, sending 25 to 30 percent back as returns (compared to 6 to 10 percent for physical shops). For example, sizing for clothing is often variable among brands. Since you are unable to try on an item in person, you might decide to buy a couple different sizes, with a plan to return the items that do not fit. Unfortunately, several brands and retailers have determined that it's more cost effective to destroy the clothes either by incineration or dumping them in a landfill than to deal with the returned item because it must be inspected to see if it is up to standard and potentially repackaged. In France the practice has been outlawed, but this is still commonplace for several brands around the world. Next time you purchase a pair of jeans online, measure twice and order once.

Food Packaging

Think of your last grocery trip or takeout order; chances are it included a lot of plastic. About 70 percent of all packaging is used for food and beverage. Since packaging is the number-one use for plastic in general — over 35 percent of all plastic generated is used for packaging — we can extrapolate that just over 25 percent of all plastic is used for our food and drinks.

Single-Serve Sachets
Single-serve sachets contain individual servings of myriad products, from shampoo and detergent, to snacks, condiments and tea. They are convenient, hygienic and a real problem for the planet.

From single-serve drink powders, to ketchup and candy bars, we find sachets everywhere. Though made more often than not of plastic, these packages are rarely recycled. This is for three main reasons:

1 Sachets are made from multiple layers of material, which can include different types of plastic and even materials such as aluminum and paper. It is possible to separate these layers but too costly to be considered.
2 Sachets are generally made of light flimsy material that can easily get stuck in recycling equipment, leading to delays and expensive repairs.
3 Sachets are made of low-value plastic, meaning there is a lack of buyers for this type of recycled plastic.

Researchers have found that 60 percent of sachets are produced by just 10 companies, led by Nestlé, Unilever and Procter & Gamble. Several environmentalists and activists agree that these companies should be held accountable for the waste generated by these sachets, since they are knowingly flooding the market with their products, particularly in parts of the world that do not have the capacity to manage the waste.

Sachets in the Philippines

While single-serve sachets are used globally, they are especially popular in Asian countries. This is particularly true in the Philippines, where over 163 million brightly colored plastic packets are consumed a day.

In the Philippines these plastic packets are an issue because of the sheer number of them — almost 60 billion sachets are purchased in a year, enough waste to cover 130,000 soccer fields — and many people have limited access to waste management. In Manila, many neighborhoods do not have their waste picked up by garbage trucks, and so individuals deal with their waste by dumping it in the streets and rivers. Even if waste management facilities were accessible, the sachets are largely unrecyclable.

Single-serve sachets, like this package of shampoo, have become a serious environmental issue in the Philippines and other Asian countries.

Swaps and Substitutes: Buy Big

Multinational corporations will argue that sachets provide low-income customers with high-quality goods that they otherwise couldn't afford. But is this true? In actuality, buying sachets on a daily basis is more expensive than buying in larger quantities (but with less waste). This false argument is less about improving quality of life and more about increasing profit.

Plastic Wrap

When plastic wrap was first discovered in the 1930s it was a mistake — a sticky residue trapped inside a beaker. Each year, Americans use enough plastic wrap to wrap the state of Texas. Over a six-month period, 80 million Americans will work their way through one roll.

If you used up a 150-meter (492-foot) roll of plastic wrap every six months, you would use **160 rolls** of wrap in a lifetime.

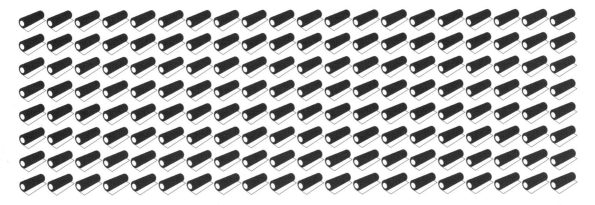

=

That equals **24 kilometers (14.9 miles)** of plastic, which is equivalent to **60 laps around a standard track**.

However, an estimated five million Americans go through 10 rolls a year. If you are one of these super wrappers, that adds up to 800 rolls or 120 kilometers (74.6 miles) of plastic wrap in a lifetime.

This thin material is discouraged from being recycled as it can jam machines. Additionally, plastic wrap is made mostly from PVC. This type of plastic releases harmful dioxins into the environment when left in a landfill or burned in an incinerator.

Swaps and Substitutes: Reusable Wraps and Containers

Go with reusable packaging. Try glass containers or reusable wraps, such as beeswax wraps, which can be washed and used again and again.

Meal Kits

Meal kits have become an increasingly popular way to cook meals at home. Every ingredient for a dish is delivered premeasured and individually packaged, which means a lot of plastic. One purchaser weighed out the plastic in a Blue Apron meal kit (containing three meals) and calculated 108 grams (3.6 ounces). According to a Nielsen Report, 14.3 million households purchased kits in the last six months of 2018. Using the Blue Apron meal kit as a base weight metric, that would add up to 1,544,400 kilograms (3,404,819 pounds) of plastic — just in one week! This waste doesn't even include the freezer bags that come inside each kit.

On the surface, it appears that meal kits are an unsustainable option because of the sheer volume of plastic packaging, but could they actually be "greener" than grocery shopping? Researchers at the University of Michigan's Center for Sustainable Systems investigated five different recipes. These included a pasta dish, a salmon dish and a cheeseburger. The researchers made each dish twice, once from ingredients bought at a grocery store and once from a meal kit. They then evaluated the greenhouse gas produced at each step of the

Meal kit ingredients are individually packaged, often in plastic.

meal: growing the food, transporting ingredients, packaging and any food waste created. From this analysis they found that on average groceries produced about 33 percent more emissions than the meal kits. This was mainly because the pre-portioned servings in the meal kits made less food waste than the grocery store.

This study is an excellent reminder to carefully evaluate your swaps and substitutes. Sometimes waste is highly visible (like in a meal kit), but in other cases we might be less aware of the waste created, though its impact is more significant.

Takeout

Takeout is any food or drink available for immediate consumption after purchase, and ordering takeout has increasingly become a part of our modern lifestyle. It's anticipated that by 2025 the global online food delivery market will be valued at $200 billion from the surge of popularity in online food ordering platforms and apps.

In Canada, 54 percent of Canadians eat out at least once a week, whether it's at a restaurant or ordering takeout. If you ordered takeout once a week and every week it comes in a 670 milliliter (22.7 fluid ounce) polypropylene container, which weighs on average 28 grams (1 ounce), including the lid, in a year you would use 1.4 kilograms (3 pounds) of plastic.

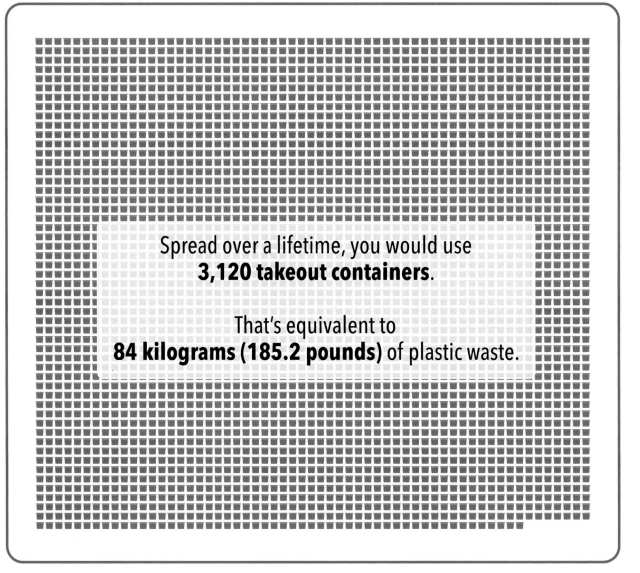

Spread over a lifetime, you would use **3,120 takeout containers**.

That's equivalent to **84 kilograms (185.2 pounds)** of plastic waste.

Food Delivery Apps in China

Like in so many parts of the world, the takeout business in China is booming, but at a price to the environment. Researchers estimate the online takeout business in China created 1.45 million metric tons of packaging waste in 2017. The industry has grown so rapidly that it created nine times more waste than just two years earlier. This waste includes over 1.2 million metric tons of plastic containers, 140,000 metric tons of plastic bags and 40,000 metric tons of plastic spoons. One of the most popular online apps, Meituan, delivered 6.4 billion food orders in 2018 — more than a 50 percent jump from 2017. If this sounds overwhelming to you, keep in mind that China creates over two times less waste per capita than the United States (1.1 kilograms/2.42 pounds per day per person in China, compared with 2.58 kilograms/5.69 pounds in America). China also recycles more of its waste than the U.S., though a lot of this recycling relies on individual garbage collectors and waste pickers.

A couple problems exist with China's recycling system. Since takeout containers need to be

A Meituan delivery person with a bag of takeout food in Shenzhen, China.

washed and are so light, pickers need to gather a huge number to make it worth the effort. Half a day's work might result in a few pennies, and so takeout containers, though recyclable, usually end up in the landfill. Another problem is many regions across China have limited formal waste management facilities, so a lot of waste escapes into the environment. Over 15 million metric tons of plastic flows into the ocean from the Yangtze River alone. This estimate, though, is using 2015 data. With the recent surge in takeout waste, this number may now be higher.

This number isn't even factoring in the plastic cutlery, straws and individual sachets for sauces. And then there is the plastic bag, which is often double-bagged to prevent leaks.

A 2018 study investigated the varying impact of three types of takeout containers: extruded polypropylene, extruded polystyrene and aluminum. Instead of investigating just one impact (such as recyclability), the researchers assessed 12 variables across each container's life cycle. Impacts included climate change, depletion of natural resources and marine ecotoxicity. The results found that polypropylene containers created the largest negative impact on the environment for seven out of the 12 variables, including climate change. Overall polystyrene had the least impact because it requires less energy to manufacture, both in terms of material and electricity requirements. However, most municipalities are unable to recycle polystyrene containers, so they are not a sustainable option either.

Swaps and Substitutes: Eat In or Come Prepared

Next time you're eating out, consider eating in the restaurant. If you have the time, having your order "for here" can reduce a lot of waste. Of course, this isn't always an option, so here are a few things to keep in mind the next time you order takeout:

- **Carry your own utensils**. If you are grabbing food on the go, having your own knife and fork can save the need for plastic ones. You don't need a fancy bamboo set, just a regular set from home will do.
- **Carry your own handkerchief**. Why not wrap your utensils in your very own handkerchief? That way you can skip a paper napkin or wet wipe (which is always wrapped in plastic). Simply throw your handkerchief in the wash at home.
- **Bring your own container**. Not all establishments will be on board with this idea, but ask the restaurant if it is able to put your food in your own container. You can try this out at your grocery store as well. Buying chicken? Ask the butcher to put your meat directly into your own container instead of wrapping it up in plastic and waxed paper.
- **Make a request**. Often with takeout and fast food you don't pick what goes in your bag; plastic utensils, condiments and napkins are thrown in with the order whether you ask for them or not. You can request that these items not be included. Some online order services have included an option to "skip the utensils" at checkout. In one year, giving consumers this option saved American takeout food delivery company Seamless over 1 million napkins and utensils!

Making a habit of carrying reusable items, such as a coffee cup, a container and cutlery, can help cut down on the need to take single-use plastic with your takeout order.

From the packaging to the products, pads and tampons use a lot of plastic.

Menstrual Products

Between puberty and menopause, half of the world's population experiences menstruation. This monthly event also comes with a lot of plastic waste.

One study surveyed 250 women and found that during their menstrual cycles 19 percent use pads only, 29 percent use tampons only and 52 percent use both. One conservative estimate states that the average woman uses five panty liners and 20 tampons per cycle, assuming her cycle lasts five days and she changes her tampon every six hours. Using this estimate, the average menstruator runs through 240 tampons and 60 pads per year.

Tampons and pads weigh 4 grams (0.14 ounces) and 5 grams (0.18 ounces), respectively. Of that mass, the bulk is plastic. Though tampons are comprised of several materials, they are wrapped in plastic, the applicator is plastic, the strings are plastic and the tampon itself is often a mix of synthetic and natural fibers. Meanwhile, pads are also wrapped in layers of plastic, use plastic adhesives to stay in place and include a leak-proof plastic barrier and absorbent petroleum-based polymers. Since these products are considered medical waste very little of it is recycled, and the bulk is disposed of in landfills.

In 2018, Americans purchased 5.8 billion tampons. That resulted in 23.2 million kilograms of waste.

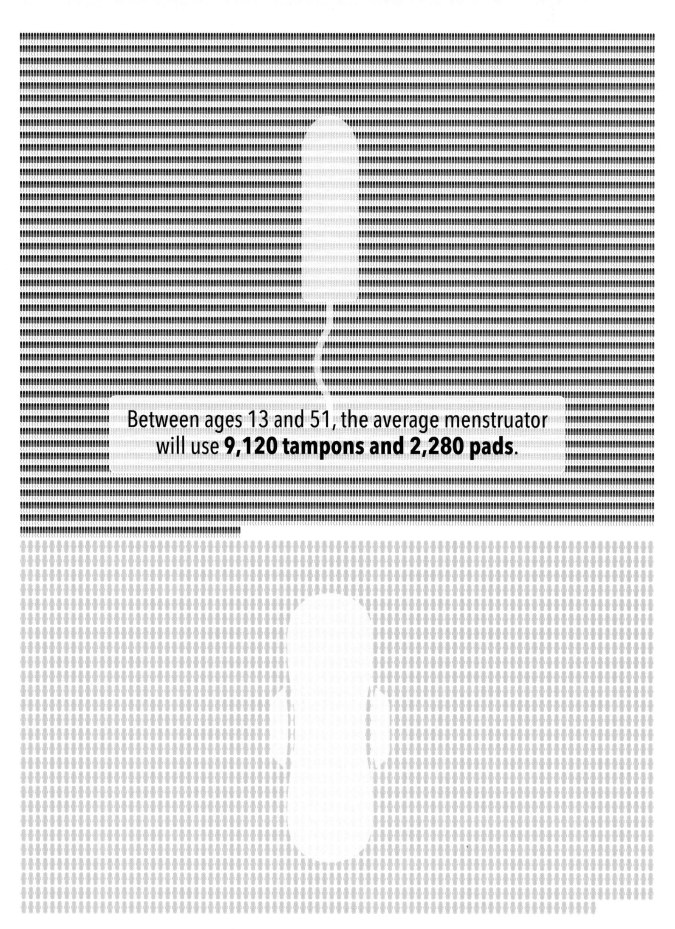

Between ages 13 and 51, the average menstruator will use **9,120 tampons and 2,280 pads**.

That's equivalent to nearly
50 kilograms (110 pounds) of plastic waste.

Swaps and Substitutes: Alternative Menstrual Products

Within the past few years dozens of menstrual products have come on the market, so if you are looking to make a change you are in luck. However, there are some sustainable options that have been around for decades. A tampon without an applicator or one that uses a cardboard applicator will minimize a substantial amount of plastic waste. In terms of reusable options, a menstrual cup, which is a nonabsorbent cup inserted into the vagina, is a widely available option. Though often made of plastic, the same cup can be used for multiple years and can be worn up to 12 hours at a time. This not only reduces waste but can also save you money and reduce your chances of leaks. Other alternatives include reusable pads, such as those made of cotton, which can be washed again and again. A more recent invention is "period panties." These undergarments are engineered with multiple layers of special fabrics designed to pull liquid away from the body and trap it inside the underwear to prevent leaks. The fabrics are mostly polymer-based and, therefore, still contribute to plastic waste, especially if you use them only for a few cycles. But if used over years, you would reduce your waste volume substantially.

Still, there is cause for concern around any type of menstrual product because the industry's products are highly unregulated. Studies have found that sanitary pads sampled from around the world all contain some amount of phthalates and volatile organic compounds — chemicals linked to cancer, asthma and hormone disruption. In 2020 a brand of period panties was found to contain PFASs (polyfluoroalkyl substances). PFASs have been found in cleaning products, paints and water-resistant fabrics and are linked to cancer and decreased fertility. These chemicals are likely found in doses that are not toxic, but repeated exposure can be a concern. Research the alternatives and assess which is the best option for you.

Silicone menstrual cups have become popular alternatives to disposable tampons and pads.

Health and Beauty Products

Whether it's deodorant, shampoo or lipstick, most of our beauty and personal grooming products are cased in plastic. The packaging industry for personal care products alone is valued at nearly $25 billion in sales, the bulk of which is made of plastic. Think of all the products you use in your daily routine; how many are packaged in plastic?

Swaps and Substitutes: Alternative Options

When restocking on beauty supplies and toiletries, consider these options:

■ **Solid over liquid**. Liquid products, like shampoo and body wash, need to be housed in a bottle and are more often than not packaged in a plastic one. By making the switch to bars (soap, shampoo, conditioner) you are generating less waste. Also, bars are more concentrated and can therefore last longer.

■ **Refill**. Package-free stores are emerging with increasing frequency. At these shops you can show up with your own containers, fill them with the goods you need and pay by weight or volume. If there is a store like this in your community, consider bringing your old beauty containers and refilling them.

■ **DIY**. Deodorant, dry shampoo and bath salts — you can find thousands of do-it-yourself recipes for each of these items. By sourcing ingredients from bulk or package-free stores, you can make as much or as little as you need.

Zero waste or package-free stores often have bulk cleaning and beauty products so you can refill your own containers.

Razors

Whether it's your legs, face or chest, a lot of us shave. An estimated 163 million Americans use disposable razors. Though the blades are made of metal the handle is most often plastic, and it's the mix of these materials that makes razors difficult to recycle. Leading razor company Gillette once recommended a new blade every five weeks, while some dermatologists recommend an even shorter turnaround time, depending on how much you shave, to avoid bacterial buildup. If you started shaving as a teen and replaced your razor every five weeks, you would go through almost 700 razors in your lifetime. If each razor weighed 10 grams (0.4 ounces), you would be sending 7 kilograms (15.4 pounds) of plastic to the landfill.

Swaps and Substitutes: Safety Razors

Safety razors were once the go-to blade of shavers everywhere. Invented in the 1800s, they gained their name from being friendlier than the straight razors used in barbershops. The replacement blade for a safety razor is just a steel blade, nothing else — making it a plastic-free option. Also, these blades are incredibly cheap, at less than 40 cents on average. A vintage safety razor might be your best bet as it was made with the intention of lasting a lifetime. Find a safety razor intimidating? Using a razor with refillable blade cartridges still contributes to plastic waste because the blades are made of plastic and metal, though it has less of an impact than buying a disposable razor.

Safety razors are a plastic-free and affordable alternative to disposable razors.

Toothbrushes

The concept of a toothbrush has been around since 3,000 BCE. "Chew sticks," which were twigs with frayed ends, were rubbed against the teeth. Bristle toothbrushes, similar to what we use today, did not appear until 1498 in China. The bristles came from the back of a hog's neck and were attached to bamboo or bone handles. In 1938 plastic nylon bristles made their way onto the scene. Today, almost all toothbrushes, whether manual or electric, are made with plastic.

We start brushing our teeth as soon as they start popping up, and if you follow the recommendations of the American Dental Association that means you're changing your brush every three months. The average manual brush weighs 20 grams (0.7 ounces).

> Over 1 billion toothbrushes are disposed of every year in the U.S. If you lined them all up, they could wrap around the planet four times.

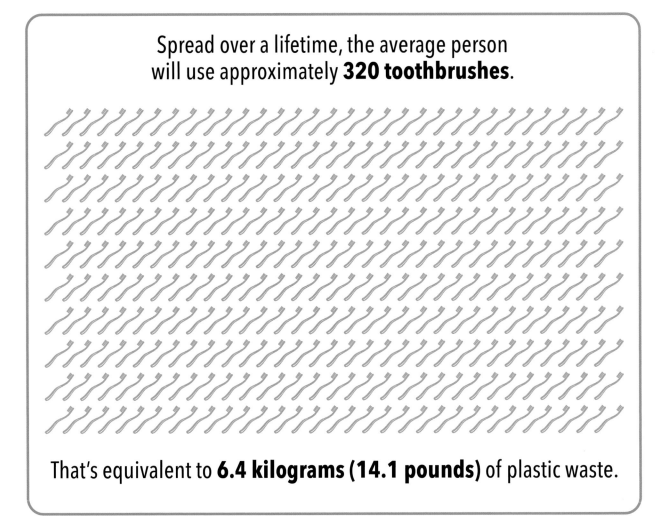

Spread over a lifetime, the average person will use approximately **320 toothbrushes**.

That's equivalent to **6.4 kilograms (14.1 pounds)** of plastic waste.

Travel toiletries

Have you ever forgotten your toothbrush while traveling and used one provided by the hotel? Hotel toiletries contribute a lot of waste; half-used soaps and shampoos just get thrown out. In an attempt to minimize this impact, hotels in Shanghai, China, are banning single-use items, such as toothbrushes, unless a guest asks for it. Hotels were told they will be fined 5,000 yuan ($725) if they are found leaving banned toiletries in rooms without request. Similarly, one hotel chain, the Marriott, has decided to stop stocking single-use toiletries and has been replacing them with refillable pumps. This change, implemented across 7,000 hotels in 132 countries, could prevent 500 million plastic bottles being sent to a landfill each year — an estimated 771,000 kilograms (1,700,000 pounds) of plastic.

Swaps and Substitutes:
Recycling Programs and Biodegradable Brushes

Though recycling programs vary across municipalities, in general toothbrushes are not recyclable — the reason being they're composed of many materials, like bristles and grips that are fused together and difficult to separate. If you are keen to have your brushes get a second life, Colgate and TerraCycle have partnered together, and you can mail them your old dental gear for free to a specialized recycling center. This includes manual toothbrushes, toothbrush packaging, toothpaste tubes, toothpaste cartons and floss containers, though the program does not include electric brushes. Alternatively, you could use brushes that break down in the environment more easily. Bamboo is a leading material, but the bristles, with a few exceptions, are still mostly made of nylon.

Maybe you could skip the brush and opt for a stick? A neem stick, which is exactly what the name suggests, is a stick from the neem tree and can be used to take care of your pearly whites. By carefully using the bristly tip you can remove plaque with the same effectiveness as a brush, according to one study. The stick is 100 percent compostable. Check with your dentist before making the switch to see if it's the right fit for your mouth. If not used properly, it can damage your gums.

Cigarettes

We hear a lot about single-use plastic bags, straws and coffee cups, but somehow one of the worst waste offenders, cigarette butts, sneaks under the radar. Maybe it's because at first glance this form of garbage — which is so small, weighing about 0.17 grams (0.006 ounces) — doesn't appear to be made of plastic. But the filter, the part that makes up the butt, absolutely is. Cigarette butts are by far the most commonly collected litter item in beach cleanups and comprise an estimated 20 to 50 percent of trash collected on the streets.

Cigarette filters have no health benefit. They were initially designed to keep loose tobacco out of a smoker's mouth. Today they are used as a marketing tool, providing the impression that they help reduce the health consequences of smoking. Filters are made from plastic cellulose acetate, and like most plastics it takes a long time to degrade.

Though smoking rates have declined over the past few decades, a lot of people still smoke. An estimated 1.1 billion people around the world puff approximately 6 trillion cigarettes each year. Of those an estimated two-thirds are flicked into the environment. Not every cigarette comes with a filter, but the majority do.

Cigarette butts are the single-most collected piece of trash on the world's beaches.

The Rise of E-Cigarettes

With the emergence of e-cigarettes more individuals, especially young people, are trying vaping instead of smoking. You could argue this switch would reduce cigarette butt waste, but this method is actually a different source of environmental contamination. Plastic nicotine pods are easily discarded in the trash or environment, while the batteries create a new stream of e-waste.

If you smoked a pack a day (approximately 20 cigarettes) starting from your teens, you would smoke roughly 474,500 cigarettes. This is equivalent to 80.67 kilograms (177.8 pounds) of plastic. If you flicked away two-thirds of your butts into the environment, that's 53.78 kilograms (118.6 pounds) of litter.

Discarded plastic lighters, like the 540 found during a 2016 cleanup of Midway Atoll, are yet another way that smoking has affected our plastic problem.

Cigarettes are toxic to the environment for similar reasons as to why smoking is toxic for our bodies. Cigarettes contain heavy metals as well as thousands of different chemicals, so when butts are soaked in rainwater these metals and chemicals leach into the environment. Studies in controlled lab settings found that leachate from a single butt could kill half the fish exposed to it — a test known as LD_{50}.

Swaps and Substitutes: Roll-Your-Own Cigarettes

If you are a smoker and want to reduce the impact your cigarettes have on the environment, there are some steps you can take. For starters, the filter has been proven insignificant in making cigarettes less damaging to your health, so opting for filter free is a good place to start. However, the filter does help keep the tobacco in place, and for this reason experts recommend rolling your own cigarettes and adding a reusable filter. There are several tutorials available online on how this is done. Rolling your own has the least impact on the environment, and you can select local, organic tobacco, which reduces the use of pesticides and emissions associated with shipping.

A common measure in toxicology studies is LD_{50}, known as the median lethal dose. It is the dose of a substance at which 50 percent of the tested population dies. This measure is used to quantify the effect of a toxin.

Plastic and the COVID-19 Pandemic

In early 2020 the world was brought to a halt because of the COVID-19 pandemic. Changes to our collective lifestyles quickly swept the globe, and some of these adaptations included our relationship with plastic. Though there is much still unknown about this virus at the time of writing, we do know that it can be transmitted via droplets expelled from an infected person's mouth (through coughing, talking, breathing, etc.) and nose (through sneezing, etc.). One potential means of protection is by using personal protective equipment (PPE). Most PPE, which includes masks and gloves, is made of plastic. Though the effectiveness of masks has been hotly debated, they are still being purchased and then disposed of in record numbers. For example, in Italy, which started lifting lockdown restrictions in May 2020, an estimated one billion masks and half a billion gloves will be needed each month. A report from the World Wildlife Fund predicts that if only 1 percent of masks are disposed of incorrectly we could still see as many as 10 million masks polluting the environment each month. A mask weighs approximately 4 grams (0.14 ounces), so this would mean an additional 480,000 kilograms (1,058,218.8 pounds) of plastic in the environment every year.

Droplets from an infected person can also land on surfaces, where the virus can live for a few hours to several days. A study from the *New England Journal of Medicine* found that the virus is detectable on copper for four hours, on cardboard for 24 hours and on stainless steel and plastic for two to three days. A separate study published in the *Journal of Hospital Infection* found that the virus can live on plastic for as many as nine days. A somewhat surprising outcome of this research is single-use plastic use is going up. Many scheduled bag bans were put on pause while existing single-use restrictions were rolled back. In many grocery stores consumers are not allowed to bring reusable bags into the stores.

Meanwhile, there is evidence to suggest that the plastic industry as well as fossil fuel lobbyists have been misrepresenting research and exploiting people's fears around COVID-19 to further their own profits. According to an article published in the *Guardian*, days after the aforementioned research came out the Plastics Industry Association urged the U.S. Department for Health and Human Services to support single-use plastics because "study-after-study" was finding reusables a health risk. It is important to note that reusable bags were not tested in either study.

If you drive, and your grocery store currently does not allow reusable bags, consider leaving them in the car and packing your items up in the parking lot. Also, be sure to wash your bags after each visit to the store. However, it's important to note that in all cases proper hygiene is your best defense against the virus: wash your hands vigorously with soap and water for at least 20 seconds and avoid touching your face. The restriction on reusable bags is just one example of how COVID-19 has impacted our plastic use. This pandemic will continue to create new challenges in our battle to reduce our plastic pollution (and perhaps create new opportunities as well).

The toll of COVID-19 has been heart wrenching and the impacts of it will likely be felt for decades. It is essential that we do what we can to save lives. However, we must adhere to the best available science and medical advice, remain critical of sources and not be influenced by those profiteering during a disaster.

(opposite page) Most disposable PPE, like masks and gloves, is made of plastic. Disposing of them in the environment puts unnecessary pressure on our waterways and wastewater treatment plants as they can get swept into sewer systems.

The COVID-19 pandemic will likely change huge aspects of our lifestyles for a long time to come, from how we grocery shop, to how we fight the plastic problem.

Calculating Your Single-Use and Short-Term-Use Plastic Footprint

As you can see from reading through this chapter, even a little bit of plastic can add up to a lot of plastic waste over your lifetime. The data we've presented is based on averages, and it's likely your daily habits don't align with them. If you want to get a better sense of how big your plastic footprint really is, do a plastic waste audit for a week.

Plastic Waste Audits

A plastic waste audit is a recorded list of how much single-use plastic you throw away in a given period. From this, you can figure out how much plastic waste you throw away in a year and over your lifetime. The keys to an accurate audit are being diligent about recording the plastic you throw out and not changing your regular habits while doing the audit.

Over the course of a week, try to record every piece of plastic you throw away, either in a notebook you carry with you or on your phone. You might try categorizing your trash, as it helps to be specific to better visualize your plastic pile at the end of the week. Using some of the categories we covered in this chapter, your audit might look a bit like this:

Item	Number per week	Number per year
Straws	2	104
Bags	3	156
Coffee pods	6	312
Cups	1	52
Takeout containers	2	104
Clamshells of produce	5	260
Packs of gum	1	52
Tampons	23	276

At the end of the week, multiply the number of items you throw away by 52 to show how many of these items you will likely throw away in a year. For items like tampons and pads, which you will only use once a month, multiply the number by 12.

You're not quite done your audit yet. Make a second list, this time of plastic items that stay with you for longer than a week. This includes plastic bottles of condiments, bottles of cleaning supplies, sponges, shampoo, makeup, toothbrushes, razors and so on — essentially any plastic items that you purchase with the intention of throwing away after a few weeks, months or once the product inside is "finished." It might help to go through each room of your home and note the plastic you interact with. After completing your second list, record how many of each of these items you go through in a year.

Once you have both lists in hand, you can start to get a sense of how much plastic waste your lifestyle creates in just a single year. Now imagine creating that amount of plastic waste over the rest of your lifetime and take time to reflect on what that looks like and means to you.

- How much space in the global trash pile does your plastic waste take up?
- Are you OK with the amount of plastic waste your lifestyle creates?
- What easy, immediate changes can you make to reduce your plastic footprint?
- What changes are more difficult to make? What makes them difficult, and are there any ways around those difficulties?

The purpose of this exercise is not to make you feel guilty about how much plastic you use; it's a tool to help you understand where most of your plastic consumption is coming from and to think critically about your daily habits. From here you can choose to change your habits and make effective, lifelong strides to reduce your plastic footprint.

CHAPTER 6

Your Plastic
Future

From extraction, to manufacturing, to disposal, this book has reviewed the many ways plastic impacts our planet at every stage of its life cycle. This chapter will remind you of some of the key solutions to fighting plastic pollution and motivate you to keep the fight going.

Keys to a Plastic-Pollution-Free Future

Below are the big points to take away from this book:

■ **Reduce first, recycle last**. When it comes to your individual footprint the first thing you should do is reduce your

(left) *Skyscraper* or the *Bruges Whale* was created by StudioKCA for Belgium's Bruges Triennial in 2018. The breaching whale consists of 5 tons of Pacific Garbage Patch plastic that was collected in Hawaii. The aim of this piece was to raise awareness of the issue of plastic in our oceans.

consumption. Be critical of the purchases you make, opt for goods with less packaging and go with brick-and-mortar stores over online shopping whenever possible. Though recycling is a piece of the waste-reduction puzzle, it won't neutralize the amount of waste you create.

■ **Make smart swaps.** When finding alternatives to plastic to incorporate into your daily life be sure that these swaps are smart. What might appear to be the more sustainable solution isn't always — so do your research. When in doubt buy items second-hand or better yet see if you can borrow them from a friend.

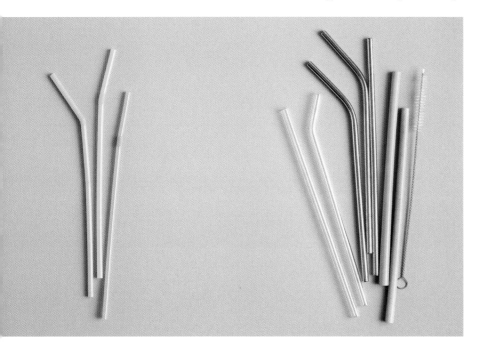

Evaluating the merits and disadvantages of plastic alternatives is an important process in changing your habits for the betterment of the environment.

■ **Add it up.** We aren't often confronted with a whole picture of our waste. When we are done with a plastic wrapper we usually just throw it away and forget about it. One of the purposes of this book is to illuminate how much your waste stacks up over time based on the choices you make. Take plastic waste audits a few times a year, and you'll likely see how small changes to your daily choices add up to big changes in your plastic footprint.

■ **Consider fossil fuels.** Fossil fuels and plastic are inextricably linked. Ninety-nine percent of all plastic is made from fossil fuels. It's important to consider not only the pollution generated from plastic litter, but also the emissions created from extracting fuels and producing plastic. If institutions and governments move their money out of coal, oil and gas, that will have a significant impact on plastic production and waste. Hundreds of institutions around the world, including universities, faith organizations and pension funds, have divested from fossil fuels. You can pressure other institutions affiliated with the fossil fuel industry to do the same.

■ **Regulate, monitor and engage.** Solutions at scale work better when they are regulated by a governing body with people's best interests in mind, when they are monitored to make sure they are still effective and when communities are engaged as part of the solutions. Across the globe some communities, dissatisfied with their government's efforts, have acted as citizen scientists, monitoring solutions for effectiveness, calling out bad solutions and coming up with new ones. If you feel your government needs to step up and invest in better oversight, put pressure on your representatives. If this is ineffective, you can rally the skills in your neighborhood to fill in the gaps.

Hold corporations accountable. Corporations need to be held accountable for their role in the plastic crisis. Plastic remains an inexpensive material because the impact it creates during its production and at the end of its life is not considered part of the price. If corporations were responsible for the true cost of these impacts, plastic material might be used more wisely. You can use your social media platforms to bring attention to the waste generated by corporations. If you see litter on the ground and recognize the brand, take a photo and tag the brand. Greenpeace has recommended using the hashtag #IsThisYours to call out brands to take responsibility for the waste they create.

Innovate. From Seabins to containers made from mushroom roots, our ability to innovate and problem solve is part of what makes us wonderfully human. With continued creativity, we will keep generating solutions to curb plastic waste. If you know of any start-up organizations doing great work to minimize plastic waste, support them if you can by either investing in their business or sharing their initiative with others.

Engage in collective action. Though our individual actions matter, even more is accomplished when we work together. Finding solutions that can be scaled up is key. Not sure where to begin? Lean on existing eco-minded clubs and organizations in your community. Chances are members within those clubs are engaged citizens who have connections with local businesses and governments, and a willingness to help.

Thousands protest at the Time Is Now demonstration in London, UK, on June 26, 2019. Protesters, descending on the streets near parliament, demanded action by the government on climate change.

A humpback whale and her calf cruise the Pacific Ocean.

Reasons to Be Hopeful

After reading through this book, you might be worried our civilization will never be able to pull ourselves out from under our mountain of plastic waste. Yes, there are many reasons to feel overwhelmed, but there are also many reasons to find hope. Here's a look at other environmental success stories that show the immense power of collective action.

Welcome Back, Whales!

During the 19th and 20th centuries, the humpback whale was hunted to near extinction. But today populations are bouncing back in record numbers. This comeback can largely be attributed to global action to stop whale hunting. In 1985 the International Whaling Commission established a moratorium on commercial whaling, and this pause in whaling operations continues to this day.

Fighting Air Pollution

In 2010 air pollution in China was linked to over 1.2 million premature deaths. Since China declared a "war on pollution" in 2013, Chinese cities and rural areas have reduced the concentration of fine particulates by 32 percent, greatly improving citizens' lives. This change is a reflection of strong enforcement and regulation.

Closing the Ozone Hole

A hole in our ozone layer was discovered in 1985. The ozone layer is the essential layer of gases between Earth and the sun that protects us from UV radiation. Scientist found that the hole was caused by human-made chemicals, specifically chlorofluorocarbons (CFCs), which can be found in aerosol cans, such as hairspray and whipped cream.

In 1987 the international community came together to sign the Montreal Protocol, a treaty signed by all 197 countries in the United Nations to phase out these chemicals. Today the hole has shrunk dramatically, and by 2060 it's anticipated to be fully closed.

Climate March

Since August 2018, youths across the globe have led school walkouts, demanding political leaders take action to prevent climate change. Though this movement was founded by youth activist Greta Thunberg, who started protesting on August 20, 2018, it is now led by a multitude of dedicated youths. Protests have happened in over 150 countries, and single-day protests have surpassed four million participants. This inspiring movement continues to grow and put pressure on governments and corporations to protect humans from climate catastrophe.

Climate change activist Greta Thunberg protests in front of the Swedish Riksdag on February 1, 2019. Her sign "skolstrejk för klimatet" translates to "school strike for the climate."

Your Footprint, Reimagined

You now have a stronger understanding of the impact plastic has at every stage of its life cycle. You also know how your daily choices can add up to a lot of plastic waste over time. Now, with this knowledge in hand it's time to reimagine your footprint. Think about the changes you are willing to make to reduce your plastic waste. Coming up with a plan is an essential first step, but committing to one can be difficult. The following are a few tips to help you stick to your waste-reduction goals.

Just Get Started

Don't worry about creating the perfect plan, just get started. Have you ever noticed that once you start a task your mind keeps nagging at you until you have completed it? This is known as the Zeigarnik Effect, where people remember unfinished tasks more readily than completed ones. By simply starting, you'll tap into this psychological phenomenon and find motivation to continue working on your plastic reduction strategy until you feel you've met your goal.

Make It a Game

One of the strongest motivators for long-term behavior change is play. It might be common sense but we are way more likely to participate in activities that we enjoy. So make your waste goals fun! Visit your favorite beach and pick up plastic debris before taking a dip. Track the amount of waste you made this week, and see if you can generate even less next week. Take a sewing class with your bestie and learn how to extend the life of your favorite jeans and shirts.

Plan for Obstacles

It's important to look on the bright side, but it's important to consider the challenges that may stand in the way of your success. Here's an example: One study followed 210 women who were trying to quit smoking. Some were told to only envision their successes while others were told to think about obstacles they would face and how they might overcome them. More women in the second group were able to quit than in the first. This is a tactic known as "mental contrasting."

Organizing cleanups with friends and family is an active way to help local ecosystems and to prevent trash from getting in our waterways.

You can apply this same technique to your plastic goals. For example, what is your plan if you forget to bring your reusable cup to the coffee shop? What is your plan if you are handed a straw at a restaurant?

Small actions, such as remembering to pack your reusable cup and tote bag, can add up to a big reductions over time.

Apply Some Peer Pressure

Sometimes a little peer pressure can be a good thing. Find an "eco" buddy who shares your goals and take on the challenge together while holding each other accountable.

Remember Every Piece Counts

You won't reduce your plastic footprint to zero overnight — it's going to take time. Every time you choose to skip on using single-use plastics is a piece you are diverting from a landfill. Every piece of trash you pick up from a beach is one less piece that will enter the ocean and possibly harm an animal. There will be times when you aren't living your ideal plastic pollution-free lifestyle, but be gentle on yourself. Too often we let a few missteps derail our goals. Remember, if everyone did their part to reduce plastic waste, albeit imperfectly, it would be more impactful than a handful of people eliminating their waste perfectly.

Please Share This Book

Thank you for reading *Your Plastic Footprint*. We hope you now have a lot more information and tools on how to reduce your plastic footprint. If you found this book helpful, please recommend or pass it on to a friend. The more people who know about plastic pollution and how to combat it, the better.

References

Introduction

Jambeck, J. R., Geyer, R., Wilcox, C., Siegler, T. R., Perryman, M., Andrady, A., Narayan, R., & Law, L. R. (2015). Plastic waste inputs from land into the ocean. *Science, 347*(6223), 768–771. https://science.sciencemag.org/content/347/6223/768

Chapter 1 — Plastic 101

Anderson, D. W., Gress, F., & Fry, D. M. (1996). Survival and dispersal of oiled brown pelicans after rehabilitation and release. *Marine Pollution Bulletin, 32*(10), 711–718. https://www.sciencedirect.com/science/article/abs/pii/0025326X96000276

Center for International Environmental Law. (2019). *Plastic & climate: The hidden costs of a plastic planet.* https://www.ciel.org/plasticandclimate/

Chang, S. E., Stone, J., Demes, K., & Piscitelli, M. (2014). Consequences of oil spills: A review and framework for informing planning. *Ecology and Society, 19*(2), 26. https://www.ecologyandsociety.org/vol19/iss2/art26/

Geyer, R., Jambeck, J. R., & Law, K. L. (2017). Production, use, and fate of all plastics ever made. *Science Advances, 3*(7), e1700782. https://advances.sciencemag.org/content/3/7/e1700782.full

Horan, T. S., Pulcastro, H., Lawson, C., Gerona, R. Martin, S. Gieske, M. C., Sartain, C. V., & Hunt, P. A. (2018). Replacement bisphenols adversely affect mouse gametogenesis with consequences for subsequent generations. *Cell, 28*(18), 2948–2954. https://www.cell.com/current-biology/fulltext/S0960-9822(18)30861-3

Howarth, R. (2019). Ideas and perspectives: Is shale gas a major driver of recent increase in global atmospheric methane? *Biogeosciences, 16*(15), 3033–3046. https://www.biogeosciences.net/16/3033/2019/

Nuka Research and Planning Group, LLC. (2015). *Technical analysis of oil spill response capabilities and limitations for trans mountain expansion project.* https://vancouver.ca/images/web/pipeline/NUKA-oil-spill-response-capabilities-and-limitations.pdf

Chapter 2 — The Plastic Problem

Brahney, J., Hallerud, M., Heim, E., Hahnenberger, M., & Sukumaran, S. (2020). Plastic rain in protected areas of the United States. *Science, 368*(6496), 1257–1260. https://science.sciencemag.org/content/368/6496/1257

Brophy, J. T., Keith, M. M., Watterson, A., Park, R., Gilbertson, M., Maticka-Tyndale, E., Beck, M., Abu-Zahra, H., Schneider, K., Reinhartz, A., DeMatteo, R., & Luginaah, I. (2012). Breast cancer risk in relation to occupations with exposure to carcinogens and endocrine disruptors: A Canadian case-control study. *Environmental Health, 11*(87). https://ehjournal.biomedcentral.com/articles/10.1186/1476-069X-11-87

Choy, C. A., Robinson, B. H., Gagne, T. O., Erwin, B., Firl, E., Halden, R. U., Hamilton, J. A., Katija, K., Lisin, S. E., Rolsky, C., & Van Houtan, K. S. (2019). The vertical distribution and biological transport of marine microplastics across the epipelagic and mesopelagic water column. *Scientific Reports, 9*(7843). https://www.nature.com/articles/s41598-019-44117-2

GESAMP. (2015). *Sources, fate and effects of microplastics in the marine environment: a global assessment.* London: International Maritime Organization. http://www.gesamp.org/site/assets/files/1275/sources-fate-and-effects-of-microplastics-in-the-marine-environment-part-2-of-a-global-assessment-en.pdf

Gestoso, I., Cacabelos, E., Ramalhosa, P., & Canning-Clode, J. (2019). Plasti-crusts: A new potential threat in the Anthropocene's rocky shores. *Science of the Total Environment, 687,* 413–415. https://doi.org/10.1016/j.scitotenv.2019.06.123

Geyer, R., Jambeck, J. R., & Law, K. L. (2017). Production, use, and fate of all plastics ever made. *Science Advances, 3*(7), e1700782. https://advances.sciencemag.org/content/3/7/e1700782.full

Gordon, D., Brandt, A., Bergerson, J., & Koomey, J. (2015). *Know your oil: Creating a global oil-climate index.* Washington: Carnegie Endowment for International Peace. https://carnegieendowment.org/2015/03/11/know-your-oil-creating-global-oil-climate-index-pub-59285

Gove, J. M., Whitney, J. L., McManus, M. A., Lecky, J., Carvalho, F. C., Lynch, J. M., Li, J., Neubauer, P., Smith, K. A., Phipps, J. E., Kobayashi, D. R., Balagso, K. B., Contreras, E. A., Manuel, M. E., Merrifield, M. A., Polovina, J. J., Asner, G. P., Maynard, J. A., & Williams, G. J. (2019). Prey-size plastics are invading larval fish nurseries. *PNAS, 116*(48), 24143–24149. https://www.pnas.org/content/116/48/24143

Gustavsson, J., Cederberg, C., & Sonesson, U. (2011). *Global food losses and food waste.* Rome: Food and Agriculture Organization of the United Nations. http://www.fao.org/3/a-i2697e.pdf

Jamieson, A. J., Brooks, L. S. R., Reid, W. D. K., Piertney, S. B., Narayanaswamy, B. E., & Linley, T. D. (2019). Microplastics and synthetic particles ingested by deep-sea amphipods in six of the deepest marine ecosystems on Earth. *Royal Society Open Science, 6*(2). https://royalsocietypublishing.org/doi/pdf/10.1098/rsos.180667

Lavers, J. L., Dicks, L., Dicks, M. R., & Finger, A. (2019). Significant plastic accumulation on the Cocos (Keeling) Islands, Australia. *Scientific Reports, 9*(7102). https://doi.org/10.1038/s41598-019-43375-4

Lebreton, L., Slat, B., Ferrari, F., Sainte-Rose, B., Aitken, J., Marthouse, R., Hajbane, S., Cunsolo, S., Schwarz, A., Levivier, A., Noble, K., Debeljak, P., Maral, H., Schoeneich-Argent, R., Brambini, R., & Reisser, J. (2018). Evidence that the Great Pacific Garbage Patch is rapidly accumulating plastic. *Scientific Reports, 8*(1). https://www.nature.com/articles/s41598-018-22939-w

Masson-Delmotte, V., Zhai, P., Pörtner, H. O., Roberts, D., Skea, J., Shukla, P. R., Pirani, A., Moufouma-Okia, W., Péan, C., Pidcock, R., Connors, S., Matthews, J. B. R., Chen, Y., Zhou, X., Gomis, M. I., Lonnoy, E., Maycock, T., Tignor, M., & Waterfield, T. (2018). *Global warming of 1.5°C. An IPCC Special Report on the impacts of global warming of 1.5°C above pre-industrial levels and related global greenhouse gas emission pathways, in the context of strengthening the global response to the threat of climate change, sustainable development, and efforts to eradicate poverty.* IPCC. https://www.ipcc.ch/sr15/

Savoca, M. S., Wohlfeil, M. E., Ebeler, S. E., & Nevitt, G. A. (2016). Marine plastic debris emits a keystone infochemical for olfactory foraging seabirds. *Science Advances, 2*(11). https://advances.sciencemag.org/content/2/11/e1600395

Shen, M., Ye, S., Zeng, G., Zhang, G., Xing, L., Tang, W., Wen, X., & Liu, S. (2020). Can microplastics pose a threat to ocean carbon sequestration? *Marine Pollution Bulletin, 150,* 110712. https://www.sciencedirect.com/science/article/pii/S0025326X19308689

Wilcox, C., Puckridge, M., Schuyler, Q. A., Townsend, K., & Hardesty, B. D. (2018). A quantitative analysis linking sea turtle mortality and plastic debris ingestion. *Scientific Reports*, *8*(12536). https://www.nature.com/articles /s41598-018-30038-z

Wilcox, C., Van Sebille, E., & Hardesty, B. D. (2015). Threat of plastic pollution to seabirds is global, pervasive, and increasing. *PNAS*, *113*(4). https://www.pnas .org/content/113/4/E491

Zheng, J., & Suh, S. (2019). Strategies to reduce the global carbon footprint of plastics. *Nature Climate Change*, *9*, 374–378. https://www.polybags.co.uk /environmentally-friendly/strategies-to-reduce-the-global-carbon-footprint -of-plastics.pdf

Chapter 3 — Solving the Plastic Problem

International Coastal Cleanup & Ocean Conservancy. (2019). *The beach and beyond: 2019 report*. Washington: Ocean Conservancy. https://oceanconservancy .org/wp-content/uploads/2019/09/Final-2019-ICC-Report.pdf

McKeown, P., Román-Ramírez, L. A., Bates, S., Wood, J., & Jones, M. D. (2019). Zinc complexes for PLA formation and chemical recycling: Towards a circular economy. *ChemSusChem*, *12*(24), 5233–5238. https://chemistry-europe .onlinelibrary.wiley.com/doi/abs/10.1002/cssc.201902755

Napper, I. E., & Thompson, R. C. (2019). Environmental deterioration of biodegradable, oxo-biodegradable, compostable, and conventional plastic carrier bags in the sea, soil, and open-air over a 3-year period. *Environmental Science and Technology*, *53*(9), 4775–4783. https://pubs.acs.org/doi/10.1021/acs.est.8b06984

Thomas, K., Dorey, C., & Obaidullah, F. (2019). *Ghost gear: The abandoned fishing nets haunting our oceans*. Hamburg: Greenpeace Germany. https://storage .googleapis.com/planet4-international-stateless/2019/11/8f290a4f -ghostgearfishingreport2019_greenpeace.pdf

Tournier, V., Topham, C. M., Gilles, A., David, B., Folgoas, C., Moya-Leclair, E., Kamionka, E., Desrousseaux, M. L., Texier, H., Gavalda, S., Cot, M., Guémard, E., Dalibey, M., Nomme, J., Cioci, G., Barbe, S., Chateau, M., André, I., Duquesne, S., & Marty, A. (2020). An engineered PET depolymerase to break down and recycle plastic bottles. *Nature*, *580*, 216–219 https://doi.org/10.1038 /s41586-020-2149-4

United Nations Environment Programme. (2015) *Global waste man-agement outlook*. UNEP. https://wedocs.unep.org/bitstream/han-dle/20.500.11822/9672/-Global_Waste_Management_Outlook-2015Global _Waste_Management_Outlook.pdf.pdf?sequence=3&amp%3BisAllowed=

United Nations Environment Programme. (2018). *Single-use plastics: A roadmap for sustainability*. UNEP. https://wedocs.unep.org/bitstream /handle/20.500.11822/25496/singleUsePlastic_sustainability.pdf

Winterich, K. P., Nenkov, G. Y., & Gonzales, G. E. (2019). Knowing what it makes: How product transformation salience increases recycling. *Journal of Mar-keting*, *83*(4), 21–37.

World Economic Forum, Ellen MacArthur Foundation, and McKinsey & Company. (2016). *The new plastics economy: Rethinking the future of plastics*. Ellen MacArthur Foundation. http://www.ellenmacarthurfoundation.org/publications

Yoshida, S., Hiraga, K., Takehana, T., Taniguchi, I., Yamaji, H., Maeda, Y., Toyohara, K., Miyamoto, K., Kimura, Y., & Oda, K. (2016). A bacterium that degrades and assimilates poly(ethylene terephthalate). *Science*, *351*(6278), 1196–1199. https://science.sciencemag.org/content/351/6278/1196

Chapter 4 — Lifetime-Use Plastic

de Saxcé, M., Pesnel, S., & Perwuelz, A. (2012). LCA of bed sheets - Some relevant parameters for lifetime assessment. *Journal of Cleaner Production, 37*, 221–228. https://www.researchgate.net/publication/271616071_LCA_of_bed _sheets_-_Some_relevant_parameters_for_lifetime_assessment

Dauch, C., Imwalle, M., Ocasio, B., & Metz, A. (2017). The influence of the number of toys in the environment on toddlers play. *Infant Behavior and Development, 50*, 78–87. https://www.researchgate.net/publication/321340499_The _influence_of_the_number_of_toys_in_the_environment_on_toddlers'_play

Masili, M., & Ventura, L. (2016). Equivalence between solar irradiance and solar simulators in aging tests of sunglasses. *BioMedical Engineering OnLine, 15*, 86. https://biomedical-engineering-online.biomedcentral.com/articles/10.1186 /s12938-016-0209-7

Napper, I. E., & Thompson, R. C. (2016). Release of synthetic microplastic plastic fibres from domestic washing machines: Effects of fabric type and washing conditions. *Marine Pollution Bulletin, 112*(1), 39–45. https://www.researchgate.net /publication/308736592_Release_of_synthetic_microplastic_plastic_fibres_from _domestic_washing_machines_Effects_of_fabric_type_and_washing_conditions

The Platform for Accelerating the Circular Economy (PACE). (2019). *A new circular vison for electronics: Time for a global reboot.* Geneva: World Economic Forum. http://www3.weforum.org/docs/WEF_A_New_Circular_Vision_for _Electronics.pdf

Prakash, S., Liu, R., Schishke, K., & Stobbe, L. (2012). Timely replacement of a notebook under consideration of environmental aspects. *Umweltbundesamt, 45.* https://www.umweltbundesamt.de/en/publikationen /timely-replacement-of-a-notebook-under

Chapter 5 — Single-Use and Short-Term-Use Plastic

Ahmed, S., & Gotoh, K. (2005). Impact of banning polythene bags on floods of Dhaka City by applying CVM and remote sensing. DOI: 10.1109/ IGARSS.2005.1525403

Alliance for Environmental Innovation. (2000). *Report of the Starbucks Coffee Company/ Alliance for Environmental Innovation Joint Task Force.* Boston: Alliance for Environmental Innovation. https://greeninitiatives.cn/pdfdoc/report /report_31_10_2016_1477910390468.pdf

Damgaard, A., Bisinella, V., Albizzati, P., & Astrup, T. (2018). *Life Cycle Assessment of grocery carrier bags. The Danish Environmental Protection Agency.* Copenhagen: The Danish Environmental Protection Agency. https://www.researchgate .net/publication/326735612_Life_Cycle_Assessment_of_grocery_carrier_bags

Heard, B. R., Bandekar, M., Vassar, B., & Miller, S. A. (2019). Comparison of life cycle environmental impacts from meal kits and grocery store meals. *Resources, Conservation and Recycling, 147*, 189–200. https://www.sciencedirect .com/science/article/abs/pii/S0921344919301703?via%3Dihub

Hernandez, L. M., Xu, E. G., Larsson, H. C. E., Tahara, R., Maisuria, V. B., & Tufenkji, N. (2019). Plastic teabags release billions of microparticles and nanoparticles into tea. *Environmental Science & Technology, 53*(21), 12300– 12310. https://pubs.acs.org/doi/abs/10.1021/acs.est.9b02540

Kampf, G., Todt, D., Pfaender, S., & Steinmann, E. (2020). Persistence of coronaviruses on inanimate surfaces and their inactivation with biocidal agents. *The Journal of Hospital Infection, 104*(3), 246–251.

Kögela, T., Bjorøy, Ø., Toto, B., Bienfait, A. M., & Sandena, M. (2020). Micro- and nanoplastic toxicity on aquatic life: Determining factors. *Science of The Total*

Environment, 709, 136050. https://www.sciencedirect.com/science/article/pii/S0048969719360462

Lusher, A. L., McHugh, M., & Thompson, R. C. (2013). Occurrence of microplastics in the gastrointestinal tract of pelagic and demersal fish from the English Channel, *Marine Pollution Bulletin, 67*(1–2), 94–99. https://www.sciencedirect.com/science/article/abs/pii/S0025326X12005668

McVeigh, K. (2020, March 27). Rightwing thinktanks use fear of Covid-19 to fight bans on plastic bags. *The Guardian.* Retrieved June 8, 2020 from https://www.theguardian.com/environment/2020/mar/27/rightwing-thinktanks-use-fear-of-covid-19-to-fight-bans-on-plastic-bags

Omar, H. A., Aggarwal, S., & Perkins, K. C. (1998). Tampon use in young women. *Journal of Pediatric and Adolescent Gynecology, 11*(3), 143–146. https://www.sciencedirect.com/science/article/abs/pii/S1083318898701342

Schmid, A. G., Mendoza, J. M. F., & Adisa, A. (2018). Environmental impacts of takeaway food containers. *Journal of Cleaner Production, 211,* 417–427. https://www.researchgate.net/publication/329166723_Environmental_impacts_of_takeaway_food_containers

Schwab, K. (2018). For online retailers, packaging is all about economics. *Marketplace.* https://www.marketplace.org/2018/03/06/online-retailers-packaging-all-about-economics/

Senathirajah, K., & Palanismai, T. (2019). How much microplastics are we ingesting?: Estimation of the mass of microplastics ingested. *University of Newcastle Australia News* website. https://www.newcastle.edu.au/newsroom/featured/plastic-ingestion-by-people-could-be-equating-to-a-credit-card-a-week/how-much-microplastics-are-we-ingesting-estimation-of-the-mass-of-microplastics-ingested

Sharma, A., Sankhla, B., Parkar, S. M., Hongal, S., Thanveer, K., & Ajithkrishnan, C.G. (2014) Effect of traditionally used neem and babool chewing stick (datun) on streptococcus mutans: An in-vitro study. *Journal of Clinical & Diagnostic Research, 8*(7): ZC15-ZC17. https://www.ncbi.nlm.nih.gov/pmc/articles/PMC4149135/

Tolbert, M., & Koscielak, K. (2018). *HSU straw analysis.* Project for ENGR308, Humboldt State University Sustainability Office. https://www.appropedia.org/HSU_straw_analysis

Van Cauwenberghe, L., & Janssen, C. R. (2014). Microplastics in bivalves cultured for human consumption. *Environmental Pollution, 193,* 65–70. https://www.expeditionmed.eu/fr/wp-content/uploads/2015/02/Van-Cauwenberghe-2014-microplastics-in-cultured-shellfish1.pdf

van Doremalen, N., Bushmaker, T., Morris, D.H., Holbrook, M.G., Gamble, A., Williamson, B.N., Tamin, A., Harcourt, J.L., Thornburg, N.J., Gerber, S.I., Lloyd-Smith, J.O., de Wit, E., & Munster, V.J. (2020). Aerosol and Surface Stability of SARS-CoV-2 as Compared with SARS-CoV-1. *New England Journal of Medicine.* https://www.nejm.org/doi/10.1056/NEJMc2004973

Weideli, D. (2013). *Environmental analysis of U.S. online shopping.* Cambridge: MIT Center for Transportation and Logistics. https://ctl.mit.edu/sites/default/files/library/public/Dimitri-Weideli-Environmental-Analysis-of-US-Online-Shopping_0.pdf

Chapter 6 — Your Plastic Future

Oettingen, G., Mayer, D., & Thorpe, J. (2010) Self-regulation of commitment to reduce cigarette consumption: Mental contrasting of future with reality, *Psychology & Health, 25*(8), 961–977. https://www.tandfonline.com/doi/abs/10.1080/08870440903079448

Additional Resources

Get Involved:

The Great Nurdle Hunt: https://www.nurdlehunt.org.uk/

Loop: https://loopstore.com/

Ocean Conservancy International Coastal Cleanup:
https://oceanconservancy.org/trash-free-seas
/international-coastal-cleanup/

Precious Plastic (an alternative plastic recycling system):
https://preciousplastic.com/

Learn More:

Ellen MacArthur Foundation:
https://www.ellenmacarthurfoundation.org/

Global Ghost Gear Initiative: https://www.ghostgear.org/

Mr. Trash Wheel and the Waterfront Partnership of Baltimore's Healthy Harbor Initiative:
https://www.mrtrashwheel.com/

National Geographic Environment — Planet or Plastic?:
https://www.nationalgeographic.com/environment/planetorplastic/

The Ocean Cleanup: https://theoceancleanup.com/

Plastic Oceans International: https://plasticoceans.org/

The Rochman Lab at the University of Toronto:
https://rochmanlab.com/

Acknowledgments

This book was written on the traditional territory of many nations, including the Mississaugas of the Credit, the Anishnabeg, the Chippewa, the Haudenosaunee and the Wendat peoples.

Completing this book, with a new baby in tow, would not have been possible without my husband, Fahim Kakar, my parents, Lucy Groszek-Salt and Robert Salt, and my editor, Julie Takasaki. To them I am forever grateful. I also would like to thank Hartley Millson for his design and Ronnie Shuker for his thoughtful copyedit.

Photo Credits

Alamy:
Alizada Studios: 10
Design Pics: 17
Everett Collection Historical: 69
Friedrich Stark: 84
gary corbett: 35
Huw Cordey / Nature Picture Library: 65
imagegallery2 / Alamy Live News: 121
Imaginechina Limited: 88
Jeff Morgan 06: 12
Paul Quayle: 59
Richard Newton: 33 (bottom)
Steffen Trumpf / dpa: 145
Susanne Masters: 33 (top)

Associated Press:
Gerald Herbert: 18, 19

Jane Hahn: 93
John Nguyen / PA Wire URN:43050532: 58
Luca Bruno: 36
Mike Groll: 62
Pavel Rahman: 109

Christine Figgener (still from https://www.youtube.com/watch?v=4wH878t78bw used with permission): 103

Gary Todd / Wikimedia Commons: 87

Ignacio Gestoso: 40

Jarenwicklund / Dreamstime.com: 106
Jonathan Whitney: 41

Loop: 70

National Oceanic and Atmospheric Administration (NOAA): 44

NOAA Coral Reef Ecosystem Program (CREP): 2, 42, 135

Phoebe / Wikimedia Commons / CC BY-SA 3.0: 48

Shutterstock:
Alla Simacheva: 147
Andrey_Popov: 119
AntiD: 117
Calvste: 116
Daria Nipot: 123
Dave Nelson: 112
Diana Zuleta: 129
Dixie Grilley: 96
Dmitry Kalinovsky: 118
Ekaterina Simonova: 131
faboi: 76
Fevziie: 127
Hananeko_Studio: 137
Igisheva Maria: 100
Imagine Earth Photography: 144

Inside Creative House: 146
John Gomez: 143
Johny Costa: 28
Josep Curto: 46
maramorosz: 102
Mejini Neskah: 52
mognev: 80
Monkey Business Images: 130
Natalliaskn: 136
NeagoneFo: 134
Newman Studio: 71
Nicolas Dorsaz: 53
orzeczenie: 64
pikselstock: 94
pim pic: 140
Savanevich Viktar: 142
septian intizom armedi: 90
smirart: 72
StreetVJ: 125
TanyaJoy: 126
VisionDive: 43
Vyacheslavikus: 77
Wachiwit: 86

The Ocean Cleanup: 39, 68

Waterfront Partnership of Baltimore: 67

Index